A Blessing In Disguise

1st Edition

Kristen Fox

A Blessing in Disguise

First Printing, 2015

ISBN-13:
978-0990908401

ISBN-10:
0990908402

Foxton Publishing

Dedicated to my amazing family. Thank you Tim, Cynthia and Kevin Fox for supporting and loving me through everything. I would not be here, if it were not for you three.

Table of Contents

Forward

Contributions from my family.

Written by Tim Fox, my daddy.

You are in for a treat. I realize I may have a slightly biased opinion, but I hear and see this all the time from people that have the opportunity to interact with my daughter. I stopped by to see her at work last week and I was sitting in a chair in the central office area, where her desk is located, patiently waiting while she handled clients that needed her assistance. The United Parcel Service (UPS) delivery man stopped by the office just to give Kristen a hug. He had no packages to deliver, but in the few short months Kristen has worked at this establishment she has already had a major impact on this middle-aged African American. He calls her Sunshine. The clients in the office will ask me if I am her father and when I proudly say yes, they immediately pour on praise and gratitude for Kristen. Although it may seem like I am overstating Kristen's impact, I can assure you I am not.

Why does she affect people in this way? It is because she has a genuine concern for everyone's welfare and she wants to have a positive impact on every person's life. The UPS deliveryman has captured it in a single word...Sunshine. Her goal is bring hope, healing and yes, a little sunshine into every person she meets. Kristen's sincerity and concern for others are as natural to her as breathing is to you or me. However, this gift has been shaped and molded through the crucible of pain and suffering.

Kristen has suffered since childbirth from a chronic digestive disorder, which has steadily gotten worse as she has gotten older. This condition has caused her great physical pain, but it has also resulted in psychological and emotional pain as well. Can you imagine going through your adolescent and young adult years with a condition like this plaguing you on a daily basis? Some of you reading this book can relate because you are going through or have gone through your own personal 'wilderness' experience. If this describes your situation then this book will encourage you to "press on!" despite your obstacles or challenges. Maybe you haven't been through a valley as dark and dreary as described here, but you are still searching for significance and a meaning for your life. I have good news for you as well. This book will lead you to the One that can fill that void in your inner being. It will lead you to the Living Water that will quench your thirst for eternity. Kristen has found peace and rest in the arms of her Heaven Father and through the redemptive work of Jesus Christ, who died and rose again for everyone...no matter what you have done or the pain and suffering you face. My prayer is that you too will leave your burden at the foot of the cross and receive the Gift from heaven that permeates this book.

I personally want to thank all the family and friends that have prayed for Kristen, stopped by for a visit, sent her encouraging notes or texts, or given her a call to brighten her day. We know this painful journey she is on requires a team effort, and there are so many faithful individuals who have supported Kristen for years. Your sustained persistence, coupled with our Heavenly Father's strength and grace, have been a major influence in Kristen's life. Thank you! Thank you! Thank you! May God bless you for your own personal sacrifice on Kristen's behalf.

To my daughter, Kristen. I am so proud of you! Taking on the challenge of writing and self-publishing a book seems ominous to me. You have always been a gifted writer. This attribute, coupled with your willingness to share your deepest feelings and be vulnerable with others, has resulted in a winning combination that will have a tremendous impact on all who read through these pages. You are and always will be my Little Princess. I am so thankful that I have had the privilege to be your father/King.

So, for those fortunate enough to have received a copy of this book, get a hot cup of coffee or hot chocolate, find a cozy chair and a warm blanket, and let this book pour life, encouragement and sunshine into your life.

Written by Cynthia Fox, my mommy.

Trust. Believing. Hoping. Words of life. The battle Kristen has encountered is extreme. The thoughts, actions and determination have either lifted her up or torn her down. These days, presently, she is living-NEVER GIVE UP! Why? She knows He dances over her. She knows without His compassion and kindness life would not be worth living. She has seen Him in many ways, but more recently in the 'little' things. The beauty of a sunrise or sunset. The ability to move, smell, and touch. The joy of seeing a bluebird or bunny during her day. The happiness that comes from knowing God and being known by Him. Restlessness comes and goes. Worry tries to control her, but fear of the 'what ifs' is slowly being left behind. She knows Whose hands are wrapped around her. Her life is His! She has walked many roads of discouragement but has chosen not to stay there. She is asking, seeking and knocking and she is finding rest for her soul in Him and Him alone. I'm proud of you Kristen and thank God for the example you are to me and many, many other lives. May you daily glorify Him-the King of Kings and Lord of Lords! Jesus, your everything!

Written by Kevin Fox, my little brother.

When I was first asked to write this for you, so many ideas ran through my head. I have so much to say! How could I write everything I want to say, without writing another book? Well Kristen, you are one heck of a woman. You have gone through mental battles that would wreck the strongest of minds. You have gone through pain, both physical and verbal, and yet you still push through. You have graduated from your dream college, even after spending a year in the hospital. You are still in pursuit of your dream of becoming a Physician Assistant. Kristen you have consistently gone to battle, and you have consistently won. The world has given you some scars, it has knocked you down, spit on you and it has continued to walk by; but hey, what's life without a few scars? What's life without a fight? I know that this life has been rough on you, and it isn't done yet. We are a family of rag tag foxes. We live messy, rough lives. We are always there for each other, and will do anything to take care of one another. We foster, nurture, and love anything or anyone that we come in contact with. Kristen, you have surpassed all of the expectations that were put in front of you. Everyone that is lucky enough to be in your life will leave with a full spirit of joy. Here's to the dreamers, so here's to you. Keep living with radiant joy and I will be with you. In front, to fight off your physical attackers, by your side, to fight off the spiritual, and behind you, supporting you when you feel as if there is nothing more for you in this life. I am proud to be your brother. Thank you for making my life worth living. -Kev

Preface

I started writing these essays, which comprise *A Blessing in Disguise*, as a research project for school. It was my senior year of college. I was working as a volunteer research assistant for a woman who was studying the lives of children living with cystic fibrosis in order to study the impact that a chronic disease has on their life. She gave these kids video cameras and asked them to record their lives. Then the other research assistants and I would transcribe the videos for her. During a team meeting, she asked us why we thought many kids didn't records the aspects of their lives that showed them receiving treatments or taking their medication for their cystic fibrosis. The majority of the assistants said it was because the kids were embarrassed or shy. However, I spoke up and said I believed the kids were trying to record their "normal people" activities because they didn't want to be defined by their disease. The kids wanted to show they could still live normal lives even though they suffered from a disease. Many of the other research assistants shot down my theory and said that it didn't make sense. I held my tongue because I feared if I said anything else I'd get too emotional.

The next time I worked on the videos I told the woman running the program that I could do more than transcribe videos. I expressed that I didn't have cystic fibrosis, but I did grow up with a chronic gastrointestinal (stomach) disease. If she desired, I could write essays about my own experience with a chronic disease. She agreed and I wrote my first essays for her on September 25, 2013.

From there I continued writing about different aspects of my disease and posted each essay on my CaringBridge site. For those who don't know about

CaringBridge, I describe it as Facebook for sick people. On your site, you can post updates. People can visit your site to find out about your health battle instead of you having to call, text or e-mail everyone with your latest health news. My surrogate grandma, Mel Kenaston, was the first person to suggest that I put the essays into a book. I laughed and said that there was no way I could write a book. I majored in Health Science and minored in Spanish. I didn't have formal writing training and knew nothing about the publishing process. Furthermore, I didn't think any publisher would even take a second look at my work. However, Grandma Kenaston didn't give up and insisted that I try. She told me that I could send my essays to her husband's second cousin, Janis Harris, publisher at Tyndale House Publishers. I finally agreed and sent the essays.

Two weeks later, in February of 2014, I had an e-mail from Mrs.

Harris. She told me that an editor read my essays and said I could very well publish a book, but needed to write more before this became feasible. This news excited me, but I wanted to focus on graduating from college, before I thought about whether or not I would actually publish a book.

Months passed, I continued writing as ideas came and posted each essay to my CaringBridge site. I received feedback from various people who read the essays. Many asked me to put my essays into a published book. I still wasn't keen about a publishing venture, but realized God may have a different idea in His mind and He was using other people to convey His plan to me.

After graduating from the University of Florida in May 2014, I explored the publishing world. The first decision I had to make was whether I needed to find a literary agent to help me publish through a publishing company or if I wanted to embark on the self-publishing route. I chose the latter option.

As months passed, I prayed, sought counsel and received help from many different sources. I also continued writing during this entire time span. My writing started to diverge from what it's like to live with a chronic disease to topics I was contemplating like how to find happiness or peace in sadness or the discouragement of depression. However, those essays are for another time and aren't found here.

During this entire process, from September 25, 2013 to December 15, 2014, I realized writing has been therapeutic for me. I had feelings and emotions I didn't know I held on to that I have subsequently let go of during this process. I simultaneously began praying that God would allow me to trust His absolutely, perfect timing and stop basing my hopes on grades, school acceptances, test results, etc. By summer 2014, I could feel a change in myself. I recognized that health-wise, I was sicker than I had ever been in the past, yet I was also more at peace with life than I'd ever been before. My parents and friends told me the anger they had sensed simmering beneath the surface was no longer there and my eyes held a peace they hadn't seen before. God has been at work in my life— the writing I thought I was doing to benefit others, has actually changed me.

The Disease

Introduction

January 22, 2012

It was merely a box of mac and cheese. It represented a quick and easy meal in the eyes of a college student or a busy mom, but an exciting treat for a little kid. However, for me, it symbolized hope. A reminder that someday I'd be able to eat this classic meal again because I'd win the battle I struggled to fight.

After completing my freshman year at the University of Florida, I came home (June 2011) excited to enjoy a Colorado summer with my family. I planned to work hard, so I could earn money for the upcoming school year and also take advantage of the neat opportunities Colorado presented. I worked as a CNA (certified nurse assistant), usually working six to seven days a week, six- to ten-hours-a-day. I competed in my first ten-mile and half marathon races. I climbed my first "14er" (a mountain peak exceeding 14,000 feet) with my daddy. I was at peak physical health. However, within a few months, my body changed so drastically that I could no longer complete any of these activities.

All my life I struggled with gastrointestinal (GI) complications. As a baby, I was labeled colicky. Time passed and Irritable Bowel Syndrome (IBS) was my diagnosis. The older I became, the harder it became to eat food. There was no rhyme, reason or pattern.

I have never been able to eat apples, tomatoes or things high in sugar. Digestion of these foods would cause a severe sensitivity where I would vomit for hours on end. When I entered high school, however, my food choices became more limited. Food high in fats and fibers would soon cause the same reaction. I would eat a salad and thirty minutes later I would vomit pieces of lettuce. It was difficult, but I learned to adjust. I thought I had reached the hardest point of my life; that I had climbed the mountain and could finally enjoy the view. Little did I know I had only climbed a foothill.

During the end of my first summer home from college, the pain I had when eating increased tenfold. I was forced to eat two meals a day but only in the evening. I would eat one meal around five or six o'clock in the evening and then another meal around ten or eleven o'clock at night. I only ate at night because the pain after eating was so severe that I couldn't function during the day. Nevertheless, most days I wasn't hungry when I needed to eat. I felt like I had eaten only a few hours beforehand. After eating I became so bloated that I looked like I was pregnant. Many times, I'd vomit food that I had eaten the previous night. This endless cycle continued for several weeks and I knew I needed to immediately contact my doctor.

The doctor ordered a gastric-emptying study (a study which measures how long it takes for food to empty out of your stomach) and the results came back severely abnormal. Because of these results, I had a G-J tube (gastro-jejunal tube-a tube which is surgically placed into your stomach and then threaded into your small intestine) placed inside me. I was released from the hospital a few days after its placement and told I should be fine to go home and eat and drink. However, when I tried to eat and drink, I began to vomit violently. I figured maybe my body was stressed and needed to adjust. Sadly, I was wrong. Over the next few days, whenever I tried to eat or drink anything I would vomit thirty minutes later. I had to be readmitted to the hospital for dehydration. This was when I realized I now climbed the mountain.

Throughout the next week, the doctors discovered I needed to have water added to my formula so I could stay hydrated while being fed. During the next few months, I readjusted to my new form of "eating" and "drinking." Nevertheless, I continued to lose weight and reached a state of severe malnutrition. My 101lb. frame, at the beginning of the summer, had been reduced to an emaciated 78 lb. body. I was readmitted to the hospital because if I progressed further in the wrong direction my life would come to an abrupt halt.

So now we come to the present (January 2012), as I sit in the hospital, my fate is still undetermined. I'm in an extreme state of malnutrition and I can't eat or drink anything by mouth, but I'm still climbing my mountain because giving up has never been an option. My family and friends have stood by my side helping me every step of the way. People ask me how I cope and the honest answer is I can't cope alone. My Lord and Savior, Jesus Christ, is my strength, and those I love, encourage me on a daily basis.

Many ask what it's like to want to eat but to be unable to. I crave food, my mouth waters at enticing smells, and I have dreams about being able to eat. I want it so badly, but my body reacts to food like I consumed poison. The best way to put it is this: Imagine your favorite appetizer, entrée or dessert. Imagine how it smells, tastes and looks. Next imagine eating it. Savoring every single morsel. You feel fine after consuming it, but within fifteen minutes you start to feel weird. A tinge of nausea comes on, like maybe it wasn't cooked right or maybe a bad ingredient was mixed into the dish. A little later you have full-blown nausea. Your hands are sweaty and you feel jittery and shaky on the inside. Then it feels as though someone is punching you in the stomach while simultaneously trying to inflate your stomach like a balloon. The pain is excruciating and unbearable. All you want to do is curl up in a ball and wish it all away.

It doesn't stop there. Within thirty or forty-five minutes that delicious item you just ate is in your mouth again, just this time it's on its way out of your body instead of in. Funny though, at this point, all you want to do it is vomit. You want to purge yourself of whatever is making you feel like you're in hell. You want to be far from it. Soon the vomiting stops, but the pain doesn't. You still feel nauseous but nothing else will come up. You're weak and shaking from the stress your body endured.

Then stage two comes: You feel whatever food, which made it into your intestines, coursing its way through them, as if there is something alive inside of you. Moving throughout your abdomen. As it moves it appears to expand your intestines, pushing your abdomen out, causing you to look like you're pregnant. You pace back and forth, hoping that physical stimulation will move things through quicker. It may work and it may not, but anything is worth a try.

Finally, hours later you start to experience some relief. During that time, you'll vomit a few more times. Sadly, depending on the size of your treat you may continue to feel horrible for the next twelve hours. Sure, some relief will come in four to five hours, but total relief won't happen for twelve hours, when your stomach and intestines are fully empty. By twelve hours, though, you realize your body needs more fuel so that you can survive and the malicious cycle repeats itself.

That is how I lived my life last summer. Every day I went through this vicious cycle until I got my G-J tube. Soon after I got the tube, the old cycle switched and a new cycle began where I vomited anything I ate or drank within the hour. Hence, it became pointless to eat since I retained zero calories and probably expended calories through vomiting.

I crave food every day. The body's need for food is so strong that you still desire that which causes you so much pain. Sometimes to stay sane I chew food and spit it back out to remember what it tastes like. I look forward to the day when I can eat once again and my food will actually stay down and move through my system pain-free. Whether that day will ever come is still to be determined. I can tell you this one thing though: I will not give up, no matter the pain or the agony. They say that in order to enjoy the view you may have to struggle up the mountain. Well, I'm determined to enjoy the view and one day soon that box of mac and cheese will transform itself into a comforting meal for me.

Fear of a Cure

September 26, 2013

You're healed, they tell me. Healed! My heart jumps with surprise. I'm healed? How? I thought I would be like this forever. I thought they didn't know what to do. I thought this disease was undiagnosed and incurable. Healed? Really? I've heard that before, but then things get worse. Can I believe it this time? If I get my hopes up will they come crashing down like the other times? What happens now that I'm cured? Can I ever be normal? Do they understand that I'm still scarred? Even though I may be cured, I'm still left with horrible scars. This disease impacted me in ways they don't understand! The most painful scars are buried deep inside me! No one can ever see them! If they find out about my scars, everyone will think I'm ungrateful! They'll think I liked being sick! They'll think I have a disorder that's psychological. Moreover, the psychologists and counselors I've talked to in the past don't understand either. They tell me to express my feelings and be honest. When I lay my heart bare, they make assumptions. Then, once those assumptions are made, they look at me differently. They want me to fall somewhere in their textbooks so they can consider my case another accomplishment they figured out and fixed. I pretend like they fixed me, so they'll leave me alone. I don't want to be tormented by listening to their assumptions. I desperately want someone to listen to me and help me sort through my feelings without judging. They say they aren't judging, but they are. I can tell.

I need to snap out of it, before they think something is wrong with me! I need to pretend like the doctors shocked me with their news. I don't want them to see the scars I'm trying to hide.

No, I haven't been healed. Yes, this was a hypothetical situation, but it addresses my true fears. I have pictured the day the doctors tell me I'm better. The day they finally figure out what is wrong with me and how to fix it. The day when pain doesn't encase me. The day where I'm not regularly vomiting. The day where my body looks healthy. The day when I can live a "normal" life. However, that day also brings fear. Fear of what life will be like after my disease. Some say I act like my disease is a security blanket. I wouldn't use that terminology, but in a way it does provide security.

Now I'm sure if you're a healthy person, you have no idea why my disease provides me security. You may be confused. However, if you have a chronic disease or you had one, you understand what I mean.

Why? Well, I've had my disease all my life. It's all I know. When I was a child, it wasn't as bad as this last half of my life. I do remember days when I wasn't in pain. I had to be careful with what I ate, but I could still eat a variety of food. However, those memories have become blurry. I don't know life without my disease. I don't know what it's like to not have to take medications to make my digestive system move. I don't know what it's like to eat an entire ice cream cone without getting sick. I don't know what it's like to drink a glass of apple juice without profusely vomiting. I don't know what it's like to eat a meal without being in pain. Sure, I'd like to know what it's like to enjoy them, but I'm scared. I'm scared of a cure because the patterns in my life will change if I'm not dealing with my disease. I'm scared because life would be so different.

For example, I'm not at a healthy weight. I'm extremely skinny. I've been a healthy weight in the past. However, I lost all the weight I gained because I was in too much pain to keep up the eating regimen required to maintain that weight. As my disease continued to progress, I started to lose more weight because I started vomiting, each time, after I ate. I never force myself to vomit; my stomach just constantly rejects food.

When I was a healthy weight, I liked how I looked, but I also wasn't used to looking anything but very skinny. Skinny is what our world says is the "best" or "ideal" look. Therefore, people usually commented, "I wish I could be as skinny as you" or something along those lines. I would tell them, "No you don't, it comes with a lot of problems," but they never understood.

So when I was at a normal/healthy weight, even though I wasn't overweight, I still wasn't fond of the extra weight concentrated in my stomach or legs. It made me feel uncomfortable because it was different than I was used to. I

could deal with how my legs
looked, because once they were
toned they were nice legs. I liked
that. However, in the beginning,
the weight in my stomach made
me uncomfortable. As time passed,
I embraced this as my new normal.
At first though, I wanted to have
the skinny stomach I was used to.
I saw a physiologist, who should
have helped me with these fears,
but when I shared them, he
shoved eating-disorder-lingo down
my throat. This caused me to
immediately close up.

Do not tell me I have an eating
disorder. Yes, I may have body
issues. Yes, I may like being
active. Yes, food may be difficult
for me to eat. Yes, those are parts
of an eating disorder. However, I
don't have one. I want to look like
my healthy friends. The body-
image issues result from living
more of my life as an underweight
person rather than someone with
an average weight. Hence, when
I'm at a normal weight I feel big,

because I'm used to being so skinny. However, once I can maintain a healthy weight, I will get used to being that size and it won't seem like I'm "big" anymore.

Next point, I love to be active. I have since I was a child. My goal of being active is to be fit and enjoy the benefits of a healthy life. I like a challenging workout because I feel good afterward. Plus, being active helps move food quickly through my digestive system. Nevertheless when my weight drops significantly, I cut back on my exercise. In other words I'm not exercising to lose weight or exercising while I'm underweight and these things are not true for people with an eating disorder.

Third point, food is difficult for me to eat because I feel sick and am in so much *pain* after I eat. At times, it seems easier to forego eating. However, I *love* food. I *love* trying new things. I even have favorite foods. I don't want food to hurt me or make me sick. So please, please *stop* telling me I have an eating disorder. I've heard this from most doctors, psychologists, and counselors. When you tell me this, you treat me like I have one and then I feel more isolated and alone. Even when I explain all of this to a new psychologist, counselor or doctor, they still diagnose me with an eating disorder or more precisely with an eating disorder not otherwise specified. As a result, I'm hesitant to see another psychologist or counselor.

Hopefully this gave you insight into the thoughts that cascade through my brain. At this point, I think it'd be helpful to make something clear. I'm not afraid of getting better. I don't want to live the rest of my life in pain and sickness. What I fear are the changes that healing brings. I fear that my scars will keep me from "fitting in" to a "normal" lifestyle. If I'm cured I'll lose things, which bring me joy through this battle.

One of the joys I have is actually because of my G-tube (gastric tube- a tube that is surgically placed into your stomach). Having a G-tube sucks. I can't wear a bikini without people staring. It can also be uncomfortable when I lie on my stomach or at other times it becomes incredibly irritated. However, it's allowed me to do things I've never been able to do before. I can eat ice cream, enjoy the flavor and then drain it out of my stomach before it makes me sick. As weird and gross as that may sound, I like it because it lets me enjoy the flavors of things I haven't been able to enjoy before! As long as it is liquid or melts and doesn't have chunks or seeds, then I can eat it and drain it out. Don't worry, I don't consume an entire carton of ice cream, but I do have a few spoonfuls. In other words, with my G-Tube, I am able to enjoy ice cream, without getting sick.

Another joy I have is incorporating a variety of food into my meals. When I eat my biggest meal, I eat more food than the average portion size. I eat more food in hopes that some will be retained even after vomiting. To be honest, I look forward to eating all those different foods; I just don't look forward to the sickness that comes after. When I'm healed, I'll be sad to miss out on my buffet of food every night, but I definitely won't miss the vomiting.

My goal with this essay wasn't to make you think people who are sick don't really want to be healed. It wasn't to make you think people who are sick love their disease. Finally, it wasn't to make you less motivated to help or show compassion to those who suffer. My goal in sharing this is for more people to understand. Those who suffer, dream of the day they are better. However, they may have scars they are scared to address. Suddenly, you need to learn how to integrate yourself into a lifestyle that doesn't involve your disease. It's a new adventure. An adventure that will take you to lands you've never been to and give you surprising opportunities. Nevertheless even though it is an exciting adventure, there are still parts that are nerve-racking and scary. I'm not healed, so I haven't started this adventure yet. However, I imagine the day I that I do, I will require just as much support then, as I do now, while fighting this disease.

If your friend, family member or patient was recently healed don't think your job of helping them is finished. They probably need extra support for the time being. They need to sort through a lot of emotions that are strange and foreign to them. They may tell you they're fine and don't need your help. They may act hostile, sullen or aloof. They may even cry, sing or yell. They may push you away, but don't leave. Help them successfully start this new adventure. Listen to them. Let them talk. Encourage them to express fears they have and let them know they won't be judged for having those concerns. The physical healing may have come, but don't forget the emotional and psychological healing may not yet be complete.

Chronic Disease

September 25, 2013

She stood among her classmates.
Her brown hair fell in waves around
her thin shoulders. Brilliant blue
eyes sparkled from her young face.
She appeared like every other
teenager around her, yet, she hid a
secret. A secret many knew about,
but a secret that wasn't apparent
to the world. A secret forcing her
to live life differently than those
she stood next to. Her secret
dictated how she had to live her
life, but she wouldn't be controlled
by her secret, she would control it.

Chronic diseases are something
that many battle on a daily basis.
Actually they are something many
must battle on a millisecond basis.
Children, who are born with chronic
disease, don't know any other life
than the one that includes their
disease. The disease is part of
every fiber of their body and they

must learn to cope with this disease or the disease will destroy them. Many try to tell these children that they understand what they go through, but no one can understand what these kids go through unless they are going or have gone through it. Pretending they can relate when they really can't, only serves as a source of frustration for the child.

As a result of this many questions remain: How do you understand what the child is dealing with? How do you help the child, but allow them to live a life of their own? How do you support the child and help the child when you have no idea what is happening?

I hope to reveal the answers to these questions in this section. You see, I was born with a chronic disease. A disease, that is still undiagnosed, but that wreaks havoc on my digestive system every day. A disease that puts me in indescribable pain and gives me flu-like symptoms on a daily basis. A disease, which tears my body apart. However, I make it my daily goal to not let others see my disease. I make it my goal to lead as normal as a life as possible. Why? Normalcy is on of the last strands I have to hold on to. If I can't hold on to this hope of normalcy, then I feel as though I will drown in my disease. While my life may never become normal, at least I can try and live my life as normal as possible.

Most children with chronic diseases desire to live normal lives and this overshadows their desire for others to know what they go through. This causes children to be reluctant to talk to their doctors, therapists or family about what they go through. They believe that if they don't acknowledge the disease, maybe it will disappear and they won't have to endure another test or appointment. The desire to live a normal life may also cause a child to refuse health care regimes or medicine routines. It's not that they don't want to do it, it's that they hope by not doing it their life can be more "normal." It's sometimes hard for them to grasp that not following this regime can actually cause their health to decline or for them to die. They usually only grasp the present and what they see is their friends aren't doing this, so why should they. If they want to be normal, then the first step would be to cut all ties with their disease and this begins with the medical care they receive every day.

As the children grow into teenagers, they understand that compliance to their medical routine is necessary for survival, but this understanding doesn't decrease their desire for normalcy. Adherence to medical regimes is extremely tiring and wearing on anyone. The pain and sickness from the disease are also draining, both mentally and physically. This is one of the main reasons for the non-compliance seen among teenagers. These teenagers are already dealing with puberty and their disease just adds more frustration and confusion to their life that they want to stop fighting and trying. Deep down they want to be normal and they are tired of having to fight their disease. Thus, they try to deny their disease and act normal by not taking their medicine or engaging in necessary routines. They are so full of physical and mental anguish that they can't continue doing what they know they must. Therefore, they stop. They stop in order to be able to experience, for a moment, what normal might be like. Unfortunately, in order to survive they have to turn their back on normalcy and look toward their disease again.

Most of the time, they don't acknowledge their disease in discussions or interaction with others. Why? Because they don't want to be labeled or known by their disease. They want to be known for the person they are inside. The person that they'd be if they didn't have their disease. The person they see as "normal." They don't want to have people connect them with a certain disease. They want it to remain only a part of their life, not their entire life.

Even those who suffer from a visible disease will do things to show that their disease doesn't have power over them. For example someone with cancer, going through chemotherapy, may opt not to get a wig, thus giving away they have cancer. They may choose not to hide their hair loss in order to demonstrate that this disease doesn't control them. They want others to see that even though the disease may have a big impact on their life, they are still capable of living their life.

Living with a chronic disease isn't about living the next few months sick, it's about living the rest of your life sick. It's struggling not only with the physical battle, but also the psychological battle you *must* overcome in order to survive the disease. Many people think you need to battle the physical symptoms first and this will cure the mental battle. Curing the physical symptoms will help mitigate the mental battle, but if those physical symptoms can't be cured quickly, then the person may die because they lost the mental battle.

This is the battle that drives the person's will to live. When a person is crying because they are tired of fighting and the best thing you can do is give them the hope they need to push on to tomorrow. You can give them hope by simply listening. Don't say you "understand" or you "know what they are going through," but listen to the pain they share with you. When they've reached this point, they stand on the edge of a cliff. One wrong step and they'll fall to their death. You must realize you can't do anything to fix their pain and you can't do anything to take away their burden, but you can try and help them bear it. By listening to them and giving them a reason not to jump, you show them they have a reason to keep fighting. When they've reached this point, they are desperate to be free of their disease. They strongly desire to be normal. Deep down they know, unless a miracle happens, they will never be free of their disease until they die. They see death as a release, as something to take away their pain forever. You must give them an anchor to this world.

I know I'd already be dead if I didn't have my family and friends anchoring me to this world. I fight for them, not for me. Death, for me, will bring relief. I'll no longer be in pain or racked with sickness. Death will also free me from the mental anguish I endure. The anguish that stems from not being normal and people treating me differently when they know the secret I hold. Death is not something I fear. What I fear is the pain I'd put my family and friends through if I were to die.

I tell myself, *Never give up.* I've vowed that while I can breathe, I can fight and so fight I will. I fight because I don't want my parents to have to bury their child. I fight because I don't want my little brother to go through life without his older sister. I fight because I don't want my friends to lose a companion. I fight because I want to give hope to others who are fighting their diseases. I fight because if I don't, I immediately will succumb. It is a constant battle. I don't get breaks, unless I'm under anesthesia. I don't get vacations or weekends. It's a battle draining me physically and emotionally. Nevertheless, it is a battle I've learned to embrace.

This battle is a part of my life now. One day I may be cured. As a matter of fact, there are children, who are cured from their chronic diseases. They start living normal lives, but they hold scars. Scars people may forget about, but ones the child is always aware of. The scars can't always be seen especially because the deepest ones are the ones that are the easiest to hide. Don't forget the child will have these scars for the rest of their lives. They may never achieve that normalcy they hoped to once they no longer suffered from their disease. Nevertheless, most will never mention the scars I allude to. Most will keep them hidden because they don't want others to label them. They still desire to be labeled as the person they are, not by the disease they had.

The next time you encounter a silent child, or one who talks about every aspect of their life, except their disease, remember what I've shared with you. They may not want to talk about their disease because they're afraid you'll know them by their disease and not by the person they truly are. Talk to them about their hopes, dreams, interests and life. Treat them as you would any other person. Once they sense that you accept them for who they are, they may open up and share with you the wounds and/or scars they've buried deep inside.

Hyperwhat?

February 14, 2014

This essay is dedicated to Dr. Phil Rogers, MD.

Her wide, blue, eleven-year-old, eyes looked over the simple room. In one corner, on a boxy TV screen, cartoon figures catapulted into the air as the protagonist once again defeated the antagonist. Cheap, red-leather cushions padded the wooden chair and benches. Thankfully, the padding was firmly fastened to the wooden skeletons of the chairs, preventing the cushions from sliding. She sat with her hands folded in her lap and gently swung her legs since they couldn't touch the ground. Her eyes moved in a full circle resting on the calm figure of a woman sitting next to her. The lady looked up from the pages of the medical record she read and gave the girl a gentle smile. Any anxiety that had welled up in her small body had disappeared and she beamed back at her mother.

The girl jumped to her feet as she heard her name echo across the waiting room. She found its source and walked toward the lady in navy scrubs. She felt the presence of her mother to her left and slipped her small hand into her mother's outstretched hand. They followed the nurse to the exam room and the girl climbed onto the sea foam green exam table. Her mother took a seat in a maroon chair that backed up against the white walls. Fortunately the walls were decorated with Disney characters holding balloons, sporting Band-Aids or hobbling along on animated crutches. She lay down on the exam table and the white paper covering the table lightly scratched her exposed skin. She closed her eyes, knowing the wait might be a long one. This wasn't her first time in a doctor's office since she had been going to doctor appointments since she was born.

Thirty minutes later her eyes snapped open. She realized she had dozed off and awoke to the sound of a squeaky door opening. She looked at the new doctor who entered. He was of normal height with a slightly balding head of brown hair and kind, gentle eyes. She didn't know it at the time, but this doctor would be the only one to never to give up on her. He'd become a source of hope and comfort for her. She'd rely on his guidance, expertise, and help for many years to come.

His hand engulfed her tiny one, but she kept her handshake firm as her daddy had taught her. The doctor shook her mother's hand and took a seat on the round stool, with those little wheels, which you can find in many doctors' offices. Instead of immediately examining her, he asked her to tell him what was going on in her life.

She told him about her family, about her friends, about school and the adventures she had outdoors. Then she talked about her tummy. She explained that when she ate she could feel the food move through her. Pain, bloating, and nausea always accompanied it. She would feel full even hours after eating. She didn't understand. She was confused and she wanted to feel better.

He asked her to describe, in more detail, how she felt after eating. She said it felt like a snake squirmed its way through her digestive system, biting her as it moved through. A smile played on his lips when she told him she knew he would touch her tummy, but she didn't want him pushing too hard because even a light touch hurt.

He told her not to worry; he wouldn't poke quite yet. He then turned to her mommy and asked her to give him a history of her daughter's illness since birth. After hearing the full story, from both the mother and daughter, the wise doctor looked at the girl and told her something she never would forget:

"My dear, I wish I could go into the other room, find a digestive system that matches yours and use it to replace the one you have. Unfortunately, they haven't invented that yet. I can tell you one thing, it's not normal for you to feel so much of what is going on in your tummy. People like your mommy and I can't feel food moving through our tummies. That isn't normal my dear and I am very sorry to hear that you have to endure that. We doctors have a fancy term for that and we call it *hyperalgesia*. It means you, my dear, can feel things that most people cannot."

"Like a superhero?" the little girl interjected.

This time a laugh escaped his lips. "You've got spirit," he said. "Yes, much like a superhero. Most people can't feel food moving through their digestive tract. You can feel everything. This is why it feels like a snake moves through your body after you eat. It also means that if I stub my toe and you stub your toe, it will hurt you a lot more because your body can feel pain to a higher extent than mine can. I wish there were a pill I could give you to make the pain better, but there is another piece to your puzzle that prevents me from doing that. Not only do you suffer from *hyperalgesia,* but you also have a problem with food moving through your digestive tract. We call this a problem with your motility. The stronger pain medicines I could give you would only make your digestive tract move slower, thereby, adding fuel to an already growing fire. Right now, there isn't much I can give you. However, I can promise you this, I'll do my best to explore every possible option there is, in hopes of providing you with relief."

Those words still echo in her mind, as though it was yesterday and not ten years ago. Furthermore, this doctor is the one doctor who has kept his promises to her. When other doctors have turned to psychological reasons for her symptoms, he has never given up thinking the root of this problem is physical. When other doctors have become confused with her symptoms and have given up, he has taken the confusion in stride and consulted colleagues around the country in order to understand her case. One of her greatest fears has been he will give up too, but through the good and the bad he has stuck by her side. Always caring, always comforting, always a source of safety.

Her case has puzzled him, frustrated him, confused him, but he has persevered. He has found she reacts to medicines, which should help her. Any improvement has only been temporary. Studies continue to show puzzling results, and others have given up, but he has pushed on.

Even when she no longer lived near his practice or in his insurance region, he still called to check on her and make sure she was okay. It didn't seem to bother him that she was in college and technically, as a pediatric doctor, he wasn't required to follow her. He still checked on her. He advocated for her while he was miles away and spent countless hours finding places where she could receive effective treatment or surgeries that may benefit her. Whenever she visited friends, in the state where he practiced, he'd make a spot in his busy schedule for her. For she was his patient and he wouldn't give up on her.

He still hasn't discovered a concise diagnosis for what ails her, but he has narrowed it down to a problem with the motility or movement in her digestive system. Her motility is abnormal, it's slow and it causes food to sit in her intestines and cause unbearable bloating, pain, and nausea. He wishes he could treat the pain, but he knows from experience that any medication he gives her will only make it worse. He wishes she wasn't plagued by the *hyperalgesia,* as well, since this amplifies the pain she already suffers from. He wishes he could stop it, but since he can't, he continues to look for ways to make it better.

The girl still talks to this doctor. She trusts him over any other doctor she has ever met. She consults with him about problems that threaten to overwhelm her and each time she finishes talking to him, she feels as if the stress drain away. He has meant so much to her that she wrote this poem in his honor during one of her many hospital stays.

They say an apple a day
Keeps the doctor away
But since I will tell no lie
I think that you're a pretty cool
guy
And to keep you away
Would be my dismay

You've always lent a helping hand
Making sure that I can still stand
You've listened to my fears
Comforting me as I shed silent
tears
Abandonment has never been your
game
You are not out for fortune or fame

Even though we may be separated
by miles
You still make sure to send me
smiles
Sure I may have moved to an
entire different state
But you sure didn't leave me to
fate
You called me to make sure I was
fine
That I was getting by on more than
a dime

Your duty as a doctor was over
But you treated me like I was a
four-leaf clover
You saw me when I wasn't under
your care
To make sure that I was still fair
But in reality I was going down
And you realized that soon I could
drown

So you worked your doctor magic
To keep my life from turning tragic
You interceded on my behalf
So that I would still be able to
laugh
You took time out of your precious
day
To make sure on this earth I would
stay

How can I ever thank you
I really have no clue
Words will never be enough
To say they are would just be some
bluff
You will always hold a special place

in my heart
But let me tell you, you've been
there from the start

So far, she hasn't met another doctor who is even a mere shadow of the greatness of this one. She knows that her time with him draws to an end, since her medical case has advanced out of the scope of his expertise as a pediatric doctor. However, he will always hold a place in her heart. He will always be a man she looks up to. She wishes there were more doctors like him in this world. Doctors who take the time to listen to their patients, never give up on them, and who go above and beyond their call of duty.

Dancing with Disorder

September 29, 2013

The fingernails of confusion buried themselves into the depths of my brain. The fires of doubt seared through my skull. The lies of insecurity swarmed in my head. Hot tears traced treacherous tracks down my cheeks. I wanted to escape, but didn't know how to. I rolled out of my bed and crawled beneath it. I laid my head against the scratchy carpet, desperate to hear my parents' voices from the kitchen beneath my bedroom.

I heard them talking and wanted them to come check on me. I couldn't call them. I couldn't admit I needed them, but I needed them more than ever. I needed their arms to wrap around me and hold me. I needed them to explain what was happening. Nevertheless, I couldn't call for them. That would admit I had a weakness and I

couldn't do that. I started tapping
the floor, and kept tapping until I
heard a knock on my door. I froze.
Wait, I didn't want them to come in
and see me like this. I was torn,
hurt, confused and afraid. Yet, I
remained frozen and silent.
Inwardly, I begged the knocker to
open the door. Another knock. I
stayed silent. I heard the sound of
footsteps fading from the door and
the tears poured. I started tapping
again. Then suddenly a sliver of
light pierced the darkness of my
room. The door had opened!

I froze again, silently coaxing my
father into my room. I saw his
feet. Heard him pat the bed and
hesitantly called my name. I didn't
answer. His voice sounded full of
pain. Then I saw his face. His eyes
were full of so much compassion
and love. I turned away, but inside
I begged him to pull my out from
under the bed and hold me in his
strong arms. I couldn't show him I
wanted him to hold me, but I
desperately did. He spoke softly,

gently to my. Asking me "What was wrong? Was I okay? What was going on?" I said nothing. Then after what seemed like a decade I felt his hand start to stroke my back and he began to sing a lullaby. "Swing low, sweet chariot..." I could no longer hold in the sobs and my chest shook. He stopped singing and said, "My little princess, what is wrong. What has someone said to you? How has someone hurt you?" I couldn't speak for the cries of my anguish were too deep. Slowly he pulled me out from under the bed. His strong arms encircled me and I buried my face deep into his shoulder. I was full of so much pain. How had it ever started?

It all began with my disease. The disease I was born with, but continued to change as the years passed. It drained me, but I always persevered. The most recent change was that every time I ate, it hurt. It was as if the food turned to poison and grew claws, so as it moved through my digestive track I'd become engulfed in pain and be overwhelmed by nausea. The doctors couldn't figure out what caused these symptoms and none of the medications worked. I decided I'd experiment on my own.

I found when I ate less food, there was less pain and nausea. I also found when I exercised or moved around the pain and nausea would disappear. Occasionally, the nausea lingered, but the pain would pretty much disappear. *Yay! Problem solved,* I thought. All I had to do was stay active and eat less food. Sadly, contrary to my belief, the problem was far from solved and this actually created more problems. Then another factor placed its cards on the table.

This factor was self-image. I was halfway through my freshman year of high school. I made friends and classes were fine, but high school was so different. I had been home-schooled all my life. Hence, I began to learn many new things about the world. Things I had been oblivious to before. On top of this I had just begun my journey through the teenage years. I was starting puberty, which came with new emotions and thoughts that burned through me. I began searching for my identity. This involved creating an image for myself; a physical image and a mental one. I was no longer a child, and as I began my transformation into adulthood, I paid close attention to the opinions of others that swirled around me.

A common topic everyone talked about was how they wanted to be skinny and lose weight. Not just people at school—people *everywhere.* The magazines pictured it, the TV screamed it, and strangers broadcasted it. Skinny was in and fat was out. I wasn't fat by any means. Actually I was relatively thin for my age and height. I wasn't underweight, but I was on the low-end of normal. I heard people tell me they wished they were as skinny as me and those words made me feel good. Therefore, I never had a goal to lose weight, but the solution I came up with to "solve" my stomach problems caused pounds to fly off my already skinny frame.

At first I actually liked it. I felt like I had achieved a goal of some sort. A goal I never set for myself, but a goal a majority of people had—the goal of losing weight. In a weird sense, I felt like the victor of a battle I had never begun. It made me feel good inside, but a ring of doubt encircled the good. My parents told me I ate too little, burned too many calories through exercise and continued to lose too much weight. Their warnings made me worried on the inside, but I didn't want to heed them. I liked this newfound control I had over my body. I decided I'd step-up my game a notch. I would do more exercise plus eat less food. *See if anyone can beat that,* I thought. The advancement onto this new playing field wreaked havoc on my life.

I began comparing myself to everyone around me. Particularly my family, since I was around them the most. If they went up the stairs in my house once, then I needed to go up them twice. If they skipped a meal, then I needed to skip a meal. You get the picture. Shortly after beginning this new game, I became filled with rage, confusion, hurt, pain, frustration, and a variety of other emotions. I felt disconnected from my family. I felt like this game had started to get out of control. I wanted to stop playing it, but my competitive nature wouldn't allow it. I must continue! Besides, I reasoned, it made my stomach hurt less, so obviously I couldn't stop now.

Unfortunately new emotions started to emerge. Emotions like anger, frustration, impatience, depression etc. overflowed too many times. I began to attack my family, because I knew that no matter what they'd still love me. I attacked them because I knew they'd never abandon my. Outwardly, I'd push them away, but inwardly I'd beg them to stay. I was hostile and sullen. I retreated under my bed on several occasions, for it was the only way I felt I could ask for comfort without actually voicing my desire. My game had started to destroy the priceless things in my life, like my health, my family and my mind.

One day, I woke up and looked in the mirror, as I got dressed. I could clearly see my ribs and my heart leapt in fear. I looked so skinny. Yet wedged in the middle of that fear was a sliver of satisfaction. A very twisted sliver, but it was there, nonetheless. I had a doctor appointment that week. I knew deep down I needed to say something. I knew I couldn't continue like this. I knew I needed help before I became so emaciated that I died from malnutrition. That ugly, twisted sliver of satisfaction tried to convince me that I should stay quiet, but I was a smart girl, and for the first time in a few months common sense would win.

At my doctor appointment I explained the pain and nausea I had. I explained how being active and eating less helped cure those symptoms. However, I was scared because I had lost a lot of weight. I asked how they feed patients who are in a coma. Couldn't they do the same for me? The doctors told me they could place an NG (nasogastric) tube in me. The slender tube would go into one of my nostrils and be threaded down into my stomach. I would receive formula through the tube so I didn't have to eat as much by mouth. I agreed to the plan.

The next three weeks changed my life. I was admitted to the hospital for the NG tube placement and then transferred to another hospital in town. At this new hospital, they placed me in the psychology ward. I was labeled with an eating disorder. I was hurt, confused and sad. I hadn't agreed to this. *Why had they placed me in a psych ward with a bunch of crazy people? I wasn't crazy! I didn't have an eating disorder—did I?* I had read about people who had eating disorders and I didn't have those same symptoms. I had some of them, but they weren't as bad as the ones I read about. I had asked for help... hadn't I?

The first day I was in the psych ward they told me I made up my symptoms and they were all in my head. I got angry and started crying. *How could I make them up when the pain felt so real? I had been sick with my stomach disease since I had been a baby. How could I have made it up then?* They also asked me if I heard voices. I told them, "Yes, your voice. What voices do you think I'm hearing?" I didn't believe anyone could hear voices, until they assigned me a roommate who actually did hear other voices. It was then when I realized I really didn't belong in this psych ward.

The glimmers of hope in that psych ward came in the form of visitors, especially my mother. My strong, able-bodied mother. The woman I had yelled at so much during the last few months. However, my mother never abandoned me. My mother told the psychologists not to tell her daughter that my stomach symptoms were only in my head. My mother fought for me each step of the way.

One time the staff tried to feed me food I had never been able to tolerate in my life. I said I couldn't eat the food and that it would make me sick. The staff said I was being non-compliant and lying. I tried to eat the food and vomited violently. So violently that I threw up my NG tube. The staff tried to claim I forced myself to vomit. When I explained those events to my mother, my mother turned into an angry mother bear. My mother set the staff straight and made sure I was given food I could tolerate. I felt safe, knowing my mother would take care of me and be an advocate for me. My mother also brought me a journal, notepaper and envelopes. I wrote many letters. I wrote a lot of letters to friends, but I also wrote many letters to my family. Begging them to forgive my horrible behavior and thanking them for never ceasing to love me. I wrote in my journal to God about finding hope and peace in His presence.

I also had other visitors. Friends, pastors, and teachers came to shower me with love and support. They helped me get through those weeks in the psych ward. My father and baby brother also came to see me. I loved when they came. I knew my father was extremely busy with work, but he still took time out to see his baby girl. He was happy to see a smile on my face. He had pulled me out from under my bed on many occasions in the past months and it had broken his heart each time. My baby brother was confused about all that was happening to his older sister, but he simply lavished lots of love on me. He hated seeing me in pain and in the hospital. He wanted to make my better, but he didn't know how, so he just loved me and by doing that he did more for me than he would ever know.

I left the hospital after two and a half weeks. I felt different, but doubt and confusion still lingered in my brain. Time passed and I gained weight. My NG tube was removed two months after the initial placement. I progressed through high school. I ate more and exercised less, but the pain and nausea remained.

I didn't want to lose weight. Actually I never wanted to lose weight. It just happened and it seemed like an accomplishment at that time. I never again saw losing weight as an accomplishment, instead, in the coming years, I felt fear each time I lost weight.

I didn't want to count calories. As a matter of fact I hated looking at the calorie content of food. Looking at calories only made me think I needed to count them. From that day on, I rarely looked at how many calories something had. If I did, I'd do my best not to focus on the number. I hated when people would say, "Oh, you know that has a ton of calories in it, right?" It made me angry because I had enjoyed my meal until they proceeded to tell me it had a ton of calories in it. Their comments made me feel guilty for eating it. I would glare at them, brush off their comment and continue eating, but it still annoyed me. As the years progressed, knowing the calorie content of my food didn't bother me as it had, but I still didn't like to focus on it.

The need to do more than everyone else subsided, but I still compared myself with others. I hated when I needed to eat more than everyone else at meals. It made me feel awkward. Fortunately, my baby brother began adolescents and, as a growing boy, he usually ate much more than me at every meal. This made me feel like I didn't have such an enormous plate of food. He helped me in a way no one else could. He never understood how much it assisted me and perhaps he never will, but it was an integral factor in my healing.

Yes, I danced with an eating disorder. It left a mark in my memory and influenced my thinking patterns. My stomach disease never improved, it actually continued to worsen. The second time I was hospitalized for my disease, the doctors immediately thought I had started another dance with the eating disorder. They couldn't figure out where my pain and nausea came from or why my intestines moved so slowly, so they assumed it was a recurrence of my past. I didn't like that. It made me angry and confused.

Presently, I wonder many things. *Can someone please understand it is not psychological? Can someone understand that these symptoms are real? Can someone just realize I want to eat, but I can't? That the pain is excruciating? That when I try to push past the pain and eat, I vomit, but not because I force myself to? Can someone understand that the gastrointestinal (G) tube I now have is great, but the formula I put through it makes me sick? Can someone understand that I chose not to use my formula because it makes my quality of life poor? Can someone understand that yes I did dance with an eating disorder years ago, but that dance ended and I have not started it again?*

Unknown

September 26, 2013

It wrapped her like a vicious viper digging its fangs deep into her flesh. Her brilliant blue eyes, clouded with the pain of her disease, peered desperately into the kind eyes of the doctor. As she looked into his soft hazel eyes, she saw the confusion he attempted to hide from her. Her heart sank as she realized even this famed doctor could tell her nothing. He'd try to fix her, but he had also encountered something he hadn't come up against before. His gentle voice interrupted her thoughts, "We need to do more tests, but there are a few things we can try. We will do all we can to help." She fought back the tears that threatened to spill over and smiled bravely as she said, "I know you will. Thank you for all you've already done." He walked out of the room and the girl felt her mother's strong arms wrap themselves around her skinny frame. At that point she couldn't hold back the tears and she buried her face in her mother's shoulder.

All my life I've struggled with gastrointestinal (GI) complications. As a baby, they said I was "colicky." As time passed and I still suffered, I was diagnosed with Irritable Bowel Disease (IBS). The years continued and time only revealed worsening conditions. A normal gastric empty studying (which measures how long it takes for food to empty out of your stomach) turned abnormal four years later. This led to a diagnosis of Gastroparesis (slow muscle movement in your stomach), then the placement of a G-J tube (gastro-jejunal tube-a tube which is surgically placed into your stomach and then threaded into your small intestine), which ultimately became a G-tube (gastric tube- a tube that is

surgically placed into your
stomach).

Nevertheless, the formula that ran
through the tube caused me to be
sick and resulted in burning
throughout my digestive system.
Unfortunately, this formula was the
top formula on the market. It was
predigested and hypoallergenic
running at eight dollars for an
eight-ounce can, but it still would
not settle in my stomach. I was
also put on various medicine
regimes, medicines that didn't
change my symptoms, but would
work miracles for others with
similar symptoms.

Since childhood, certain foods
triggered violent episodes of
vomiting. While not a true allergic
reaction (Technically, a true
allergic reaction requires an
EpiPen.), I would always list these
foods when I had to name what I
was allergic to. As I grew older, the
list grew. It grew so large that it
became easier to list the foods I

could eat verse those I couldn't.
This fact also presented the
doctors with an added challenge.

How do you treat someone with all
these symptoms? How do you
diagnose them? Can you cure
them? Where do you begin? How
do you continue when you run into
wall after wall? What do you tell
your patient when even the top
gastrointestinal doctors, you sent
them to, can't fix the problem?

If you're a doctor, sometimes the
best thing you can do is be honest.
Your patient may not want to hear
the truth, but in the long run they
will appreciate it. I have had
doctors cut off communication with
me instead of telling me they can't
help me anymore. I have had
doctors promise they know what to
do and when they can't find an
answer they turn to psychological
reasons for why I might be like
this. I want to hear one day
something worked, but I also don't
want the doctors to give up

because they no longer know what to do. I hold a thin string of hope for a cure, yet if they stop trying then that thin string of hope will break instantly and I'll fall to a point of no return.

I stare into my future and it's incredibly blurry. Yes, I have plans, for if I didn't have plans for my life, then I wouldn't have something to push toward. However, I see a blurry picture because I don't know where my disease will take me. I don't know what road I'll have to travel or if I'll be able to travel the road of life much longer. Regardless, I must believe in a future, no matter how blurry it is, because if I stop believing then I'll lose the mental battle.

In this battle, I must constantly fight. It's a tumultuous and confusing battle. A battle that many times is shrouded in darkness. The darkness of loss, sadness, loneliness, bewilderment and frustration. I want to at least know and understand what the viper is, that wraps its writhing body around me. Struggling with something that can't be pinpointed or treated completely presents challenges that diagnosed diseases don't present. At least someone with a diagnosed disease knows what is happening. Sure, they may need daily treatments in order to survive, but at least there are proven treatments out there that aid them in their disease. I feel like I'm stranded in a small dinghy, riddled with holes, in the middle of the ocean. It may carry me to safety if the patches I've placed over the holes stay strong, but it threatens to sink at any moment. Yes, I'm afloat, but I ask myself *how long will those patches hold*?

The Cycle

December 30, 2013

It's an endless cycle, which confuses me. A cycle spinning uncontrollably, spinning faster and faster as time passes. It's a cycle I'm sure I've had since birth. Back then it moved slowly. As my life progressed, it picked up speed. It gained momentum because it didn't know what else to do. It's a cycle that has become dangerous. One that has impacted not only my life, but also the lives of those I love and care about. For someone who likes to have perfect control over everything, this is beyond my control. However, the only way I can stop the cycle is to deny myself something I need- food.

I've always had problems with my GI system, but as the years have passed, the problems have increased. Pain, nausea and bloating are all components of this cycle. You see, not eating causes those symptoms to almost disappear. Eating makes them worse. However, I need to eat, even though it makes me vomit and leaves me feeling horrible, because we all need food to survive. So I eat and then I fight. I fight against my body's desire to reject food. I fight my mind telling me that I'll be free from the agony when I vomit. I fight against my entire being. Sometimes it works, but recently it has become difficult to fight against it. The nausea is worse, the pain is excruciating and I am so tired. The vomiting brings relief so it becomes easy to just let the vomiting occur verse trying to hold it off. I wonder if *I vomit because I desire relief more than I desire anything else?* To be honest I'm not sure if I know the answer to that question.

See, I love food — to eat, taste and experience it. I just don't enjoy the agony it puts me in afterward. After I eat it's like I'm in a tunnel. I can't focus on interacting with people—I can barely move or think. The pain crowds out everything else. It consumes me. It scares me. It causes panic to well up in me. My body screams at me, and every human instinct I possess tells me to try and escape the torture. Now if I don't vomit, I suffer for hours. I suffer physical and mental anguish. I feel like I'm being tortured in a cruel and unusual way. At that point all I want is to be able to escape the torture.

This cycle tears me apart and I hate it. It tears my parents apart. I see the pain in their eyes because they want to help, but they can't. They support and love me, but they can't take the pain or the cycle away. No one has figured out how to take it away. Through overeating, I retain more calories than when I don't overeat, but I'm not sure that's not the best way to deal with things. Eating smaller meals is good, but I can't keep them down. I drink liquids while eating, in hopes that I'll retain the food and vomit just the liquid. It works some of the time.

The distress my body goes into after a meal is a distress I fear. I hate to enter that cycle again. Yet every day I *have to* enter that cycle—even multiple times a day and it's scary. It's like submitting yourself to torture, self-inflicted torture. I don't force myself to vomit, my body does it naturally. It's all part of that vicious cycle and has turned into a deadly pattern that my body has adjusted to. A pattern that is flawed.

If someone watched me every time I ate and for hours afterwards, I honestly can tell you I probably wouldn't vomit because I fear vomiting in front of people. I hate to see their disappointment and sadness as they watch me vomit. I hate having someone else watch me while I'm in pain. They don't make it better. Whether it's a stranger or a friend, it doesn't matter, it all feels the same. I hate when people see what happens. I'm not sure why I feel that way, but I do. I try to protect them from the pain of seeing me vomit and in doing so I increase the intensity of the torture I am experiencing.

I feel like something eats away at my brain, stomach, body, and soul. I feel isolated, alone and far from anyone's reach. My doctors and family are there, supportive and helpful, but they don't know what I go through. They can't experience it and I don't want them to. When someone holds my hand as I undergo this torture, it only increases and magnifies the torture to heights they can't imagine. I try to be brave, but it becomes difficult. The torture I experience makes me feel trapped, scared and panicked. People want to distract me when I eat to try, but they just become an added stimulus to the pain I'm already experiencing.

Hence, it ends up being easier if I'm alone after I eat.

So I'm left with my cycle. A cycle that causes me to isolate myself and experience physical, psychological and emotional torture. Torture that I fear, will one day make me go insane.

So what do I do?

Love-Hate Relationship

October 3, 2013

Love-hate relationships—we all have them. Relationships where we love the thing so much, but, at the same time, we hate it. They confuse us. They leave us with stress, happiness, pain, and joy. Sometimes they tear us apart because we don't know how to process the relationship. *Are they bad? Are they good? Or are they just relationships you must try to work with?* Two of my biggest love-hate relationships were created because of this disease that enshrouds my body: These relationships are the ones I have with vomiting and food.

The smell of fried chicken and fresh bread wafted through the grocery store. My mouth watered. All around me delicacies screamed at me to pick them up and place them in my cart so I could enjoy them later. Everything looked good. I wandered through the aisles grabbing the items on my list and then hurried to the checkout lane before my eyes convinced my mind to buy things I didn't need. I paid my bill and left the store, but a twinge of guilt wiggled around in my brain. Whenever I go grocery shopping, I usually feel guilty about the money I spend. I know I'll eat the food, but it seems wasteful because ultimately I usually vomit up the food

Hold it right there!! I bet you assumed I'm bulimic. Hands down I probably called you out. Well, you assumed wrong. It's okay, I forgive you for jumping to conclusions. To be honest, I would've reached the same conclusion if I weren't the one writing this. Nevertheless, I've demonstrated a real problem. The problem that causes people to jump to conclusions before learning the full story. For people dealing with an unknown disease, this can be devastating. They desperately want to talk with a doctor, friends or family about what they suffer from, but they keep quiet because they're afraid others will stigmatize or stereotype them.

The common stigma attached to vomiting food is bulimia. While this is a *real* problem, it isn't one I'm dealing with. Regardless, I'm reluctant to tell doctors or anyone else, for that matter, what happens to me because I fear they'll think I'm bulimic. Too often, I've seen people place that stigma on me because it seems to make more sense than what I actually deal with.

My disease is a chronic stomach disease. One that contains many anomalies and leaves doctor after doctor confused and frustrated. The uncertainty encasing my disease leads to many doctors, friends, and strangers assuming I'm plagued by an eating disorder, since an eating disorder is easier to explain. If I'm plagued by an eating disorder, my disease simply becomes an issue to resolve psychologically rather than physically.

For friends and strangers it's easy to conclude I have an eating disorder because they've heard and know more about eating disorders. For someone to accept I have an undiagnosed disease means they must open themselves up to confusion. No one enjoys confusion. So instead, they adopt stigmas and stereotypes to help everything make sense. This way they don't have to deal with the fear and ambiguity of acknowledging my unknown disease, for which they haven't found a cure.

What they don't realize is that I battle this fear and ambiguity daily. I'm constantly pounded by an emotional storm. The seas of confusion threaten to drown me at any moment.

Picture it this way; I'm on a worn dinghy in the middle of a storm and my family is on a steady tugboat pulling me through the tempestuous sea. My close friends are on a battleship lending me aid, but incredibly safe within the walls of ship. Those who only acknowledge I have an undiagnosed disease are aboard a luxury cruise ship. The rain from the storm may get them wet, but otherwise they're comfortable. Those who believe I have a problem, but don't want to invest time or effort into figuring it out or supporting me are in a submarine. They escape below the storm and pretend it doesn't exist. Finally, there are those who don't believe me and choose to listen to the stigmas and stereotypes. These people are the ones sitting on their couches, far from the storm, watching the events unfold on their TV screens. They see blue skies outside so it's hard for them to believe the storm exists.

As test results come back inconclusive and my health continues downhill, more people return home to the comfort of their couches. They're afraid to stay on this stormy sea. They retreat to what they know because there is no fear or ambiguity. I don't have this option. My dinghy wouldn't stay afloat if it weren't for the strong rope anchoring it to the tugboat. My family has no other option because they know if they abandon ship then I'll sink. Everyone else has a choice. They don't want to weather the storm anymore so they retreat. I don't expect anyone to be in the dinghy with me, I only desire support from the other ships out in the sea with me.

My second love-hate relationships is with food. I love food. I love trying new foods. I love the taste of a hot biscuit layered with butter, melting in my mouth. I love the fluffiness of whipped cream cheese, the blend of flavors in a sausage, egg and cheese breakfast sandwich, the creaminess of Alfredo sauce, the heartiness of fresh bread. It all tastes delicious and I look forward to eating it—until it enters my stomach.

Usually within ten minutes of eating anything I'm attacked. It feels like three big, strong men have jumped me and have pummeled my abdomen and head with their rock hard fists. The food I ate seems to have turned into a poisonous snake. It writhes its way through my digestive system. Inserting its deadly fangs into the tender muscles of my digestive track. They pierce my soft flesh resulting in sharp and burning pain. It takes all the self-control in me not to scream and cry. As time passes, nausea seeps in through the wounds I sustained. My muscles convulse and I start to tremble, as the meal I just ate begins to exit by the way it came in. Finally, an hour later I lay exhausted in bed. My abdomen throbs, but the pain is less. The nausea abates, fading slowly as the minutes pass. I sigh in relief and lay there waiting for sleep to release me from the pain that remains. Interestingly enough, as I lay there, I sometimes will contemplate my next meal and a small part of me looks forward to the brief enjoyment it will bring.

So you see, I *love* food, but *hate* what it does to me. I have been plagued by food all my life, even when I was a baby. From infancy to the present, every meal elicits pain, but the degree of pain will vary. Desperate thoughts accompany the pain. Thoughts which crowd my brain. Thoughts like: *I need to escape this hell. I need this food to get out of me. I can't stand this. I feel like I'm dying. I can't think straight. How long will this last?* Even at these times, I don't force myself to vomit, but when the agony jumps off the charts I hope my body will choose to reject the food, so I can escape the pain.

Now I ask you. Is it wrong to find relief in vomiting? Is it wrong to enjoy food even though I know it will make me sick? Is it wrong to have these love-hate relationships? Maybe these relationships aren't the best, but I can tell, without a doubt in my mind, that being able to find the balance in these two relationships is the one way my little dinghy will stay afloat.

Skinny Skeleton

October 1, 2013

"Too skinny! You're ugly! Stick figure!"

Their words felt like daggers piercing my heart. I kept my head down, pretending like I didn't hear them. I gave them the benefit of the doubt. I attributed their words to their drunken state, convincing myself they wouldn't have said that to me if they were sober. I tried to reassure myself, but I wasn't convinced. I knew they probably voiced what everyone else thought. I always feel people's judgmental stares. Their eyes hold questions like: *Is she anorexic? Does she ever eat? How can she be so skinny and still be alive? Shouldn't she be in the hospital?* I'd try and meet their harsh stares with a smile, but it was hard, so sometimes I'd avoid eye contact altogether.

My body is emaciated. I look like a skeleton. You might think I'm hard on myself, but reality is sometimes hard to hear. I'm not over-exaggerating or being sarcastic. The sad truth is that my fight against this stomach disease has, once again, started to go downhill. The pounds I regained have all but disappeared. An ugly pattern has formed. My health will go downhill, plateau, go downhill, plateau and so on and so forth. During the times when my health plateaus, the pain and nausea aren't as bad. This makes it easier to eat and retain more calories. On the other hand, during each downhill, the pain, nausea and vomiting are at an all-time high. That deadly trio results in rapid weight loss.

Many doctors think that my weight-loss trend is caused by an eating disorder. Yes, I once danced a jig with an eating disorder, however that dance ended and it never started again. I'm not forcing myself to vomit, restricting calories or obsessed with exercising. I don't hide the weight loss. The weight loss doesn't make me happy and in reality it scares me. It scares me immensely!

Two years ago, I got a G-tube so I could use a predigested, hypoallergenic, high-calorie formula when I couldn't eat enough food. Doctors told me that using the formula shouldn't cause pain or vomiting. However, it resulted in both symptoms. My entire digestive system would have a burning, aching pain throughout the entire feeding process. After eight to nine ounces of formula were pumped in via the IV I would usually begin vomiting. Keep in mind, this formula was pumped into me at an extremely slow rate—approximately eight ounces over the course of an hour. In other words, imagine taking an entire hour to finish one cup of water!

Unfortunately, the formula wouldn't empty fast enough out of my stomach and I'd get sick. The only way I could keep the formula down so that I would be able to absorb it was to have the rate so slow that I couldn't receive any other form of nutrition because it took so long for the feeding to occur. The entire time I received my feeding, I'd have pain in my digestive track plus would suffer from excruciating headaches.

I eventually reached a normal weight with the help of the tube and maintained that weight for six months by eating a ton of food every day plus having my G-tube feedings at night. Nevertheless, I was still utterly miserable. My emotions seemed out of control. I couldn't focus on anything because my pain distracted me. The pain and nausea I felt almost sent me over the edge. I was moody, angry and frustrated. I wanted to escape the symptoms so I could think clearly.

Finally, I had enough. I decreased my caloric intake and used my formula intermittently. I started feeling better within a matter of days. I wasn't the only one who noticed a difference, because friends began to comment on my demeanor. They said I seemed much happier and more at peace than before.

I was happy and could finally think clearly. I didn't feel so angry or depressed. It was great, but at the same time it wasn't. I began losing the weight I'd gained back. I eventually stabilized entering another plateau phase. However, I most definitely wasn't within my normal weight range, yet I still looked healthy.

A short time later, I began another downhill slope. This time even though I ate a ton of food, I vomited too many calories. I started to use my formula again, but stopped when the formula made me very sick. I actually seemed to vomit less with real food than with the formula, so I stuck to actual food. I pureed anything that couldn't dissolve on its own when placed in a cup of water. I ate many meals throughout the course of the day. I couldn't eat anything that was hard to digest (anything high in fat or fiber). I also had to factor in my other allergies: sugars, apples, and tomatoes. This left me with limited options, but I focused on working with what I had.

I also tried to conserve energy through any means possible. I love to exercise, so I hate when I lose weight and have to stop exercising. Still, my health comes first and sadly I haven't been able to run in over a year. While many view running as a punishment, I view it as a reward. I can't wait to feel the

pavement pounding underneath
my feet again.

I also enjoy going on a daily prayer
walk. I talk to Jesus and always
feel better afterward. However,
that prayer walk has been reduced
to a shadow of its former self. It
would be foolish of me to keep it at
the length it used to be. I have had
to continue to cut more things out
of my life that I love to do in order
to conserve energy. I realize I can't
push myself right now or I'll push
myself right over the edge. It pains
me to give up things I love.
Nevertheless, that pain is not
anywhere near the level of agony
that I experienced a year ago,
when I was at a normal weight.

The hardest thing for me, when I
lose weight is the disappointment
and frustration I hear from my
doctors and family. I feel like a
failure—like I didn't try hard
enough or gave up too quickly.
None of them understand what it's
like, to try and sustain a normal

weight. Sure, I still have pain and nausea regardless of the weight I'm at, but when I'm eating less and hence at a lower weight it's not quite as bad.

I feel as though the doctors continue to give up on me one by one. They can't explain my symptoms and can't figure out a cure. I fit perfectly in the eating disorder package, so write me off as having one. I don't want them to give up on me. I need them to keep trying. I want them to figure out what is happening in my body. *If they give up then who else will make the effort?*

My family doesn't pretend to understand. They focus on loving and supporting me. However, I still feel like I failed them. They get a chance to breathe and then because of this disease I put them right back on the roller coaster that is my health. I actually wouldn't keep fighting if it weren't for them. I wouldn't fight through this daily hell for myself. No, I'd rather be in the arms of Jesus, living in a place where pain and suffering don't exist. Yet, I stay on this earth, because I'm fighting for those I love. I fight so my parents don't have to attend their little girl's funeral. I fight so my baby brother doesn't become an only child. I fight so my father can one day walk me down the aisle. I fight so my mother can hold her grandchild. I fight so my brother can take his nieces or nephews out for ice cream. I fight for those who give me support and love. I fight because the moment I stop, will be the moment my life stops. It may seem like I'm losing the physical battle, but I'm winning the mental one. I will keep fighting until God takes every last drop of air from my lungs. For at that point, He has called me home and no one wins a fight against God. Right now, though, He's still giving me air, so I fight on.

Different

Different. I was always different than everyone else. At birthday parties, I was the only child not eating birthday cake. Whenever our family got invited over to someone's house for dinner, we always brought something for me to eat, since I usually couldn't eat what was served. As I grew up, things didn't get better, they continued to get worse causing the stamp of "different" or "strange" to grow even bigger. This stamp has taught me many different things. I've learned to cope and deal with stares from strangers and my peers. I've learned that it's safest to hide the intricate details of my health from friends. I've learned that when I pack for a trip, I need to worry about a lot more than just clothes and toiletries.

At Halloween I did more than just dress differently. "Trick or Treat!" I shouted cheerfully as the red door, plastered with spooky skeletons, black cats, and wispy cobwebs, opened. I held out my plastic orange pumpkin, my blue eyes peering up at the stranger. I flashed them a sparkling smile. "An extra treat for the little angel," the stranger said as they placed a giant handful of candy in my pumpkin. I thanked them and turned away, my golden curls bouncing as I hopped down the steps. I quickly adjusted my little halo, shrugged my silver wings up higher on my back and continued on my journey. Later that night I sorted through all the goodies I received. Mini piles decorated the living room floor. There was a pile of candy mommy liked, a pile daddy liked, a pile no one liked and my pile. My pile contained a few bags of pretzels, Goldfish crackers, a blue plastic toothbrush, and a tiny container of Play-Doh. It wasn't much, but it was more than usual. Not being able to eat candy resulted in a relatively small pile. However, I still enjoyed every minute of the Halloween tradition.

At birthday parties I celebrated a little differently. "Time to eat!" the mother shouted. As all the kids at the birthday party ran over to the table, containing hearty slices of savory pizza, I migrated over to my own mom. She handed me a container of noodles and I plopped down at one of the tables. "How come you're eating that? Pizza is ten times better!" one kid stated. "Well, I'm allergic to tomatoes and can't eat pizza. Besides, I love pasta!" I said enthusiastically, but inwardly I sighed. It's tiring having to explain myself at every birthday party or dinner I attend. Let me tell you, the two most common dishes to feed a large crowd are pizza or lasagna — both of which have tomatoes listed as on of their main ingredients.

At sleep-away camps I had to do things a little different. "I'll shake it up for you." I looked up at the camp counselor who stood above me. I had retreated to a corner so I could mix my medicine without attracting the stares from other campers. I knew they still watched me, but at least with my back turned they couldn't see what I was doing. Unfortunately, their stares still drilled holes in my back. "Thanks, but I'm used to it." I told the counselor. Taking medicine multiple times a day was something I'd grown up with and knew I had to stick with, whether I was at home, school or even at an overnight camp.

When I at a friend's house I had to act differently. "I almost ate a whole banana today!" I told my mother proudly. She looked at my eager blue eyes and saw a glimmer of hesitation in them. "But..." she prodded. I looked away and felt a tear trace a warm track down my cheek. "But I threw it up," I sobbed. My mother picked up my five-year-old frame and held me in her arms. "It's okay my little angel, it's not your fault." I knew she was right. My tears, though, stemmed mainly from the fact that I couldn't be like other kids. They ate fruit every day. *Why couldn't I?*

My food and sweets pallet was much different than other peoples' pallets. "Please take your seats and buckle up for landing," the flight attendant announced over the loud speaker. I barely heard her because my face was buried in an airsick bag. My mother held the white paper bag in one hand and with the other hand she attempted to open another bag. The third person in our row, an elderly lady, crooned in sympathy. I wasn't vomiting because of the airplane's descent. No, I was vomiting because I'd eaten a few cookies and part of a candy bar. The friends I made on the plane, during the long flight to Hawaii had shared their goodies with me. I had eagerly accepted the treats, but knew in the back of my head I probably shouldn't have. *But I was on vacation, right?* The treats were absolutely marvelous, but within ten minutes I had to run back to my seat. My mother saw the frantic look on my face and knew before I even spoke that she needed to open that vomit bag immediately. Once again, I tried to defy my allergies and they got the best of me.

As a victim of a chronic disease, I have had to travel a different road of life. This road is incredibly windy and contains numerous roadblocks, potholes, and hills. It's a road traveled by few, but I while I travel my road I am able to observe from afar, the road most travel. It looks much smoother, wider and more inviting than my road. I've tried to venture in that direction, but I can't. It's like there is an invisible barrier between these roads, a barrier that forces me to stay on my road. However, those on the "healthy" road are able to cross over to my road. When they come they offer encouragement and support to me. Few have crossed over, but the few that have, are the ones who have made the most impact on my life. No one walks my road all the time, but there are those who often join me because they don't want to see me walk alone. When they walk with me, they see glimpses of my pain and also gain insight to how I've navigated this road my entire life.

My ever-present Guide is the true reason I've been able to navigate this road. A Man with a soft and kind face, eyes full of grace, leading me through the maze that dominates my road. He has never led me in the wrong direction. Most of the time, He carries me in His strong arms, caressing my hair with His gentle hands, which contain holes from where ugly nails pierced them.

My family and closest friends are the ones who have dared to cross over to my road and travel parts of it with me. Some friends have ventured over, but once they see the terror it holds, they run back to the safety of their road. Some say they'll come and travel my road with me one day, but I still wait for that day to come. I no longer get mad when friends desert me or when people who said they'd be there through thick and thin, leave long before the thin even occurs. I understand my life contains so many anomalies and ambiguities. I know this elicits fear in many hearts. I understand they leave in order to protect themselves. Nevertheless, their leaving still causes me pain.

Pain because I don't know if I'll ever be normal. Pain because I may have to travel this road for the rest of my life. Pain because I want them to understand I don't need them to solve my problem, I only need their support and company. Without their support, it becomes easier for me to stumble as I walk.

When I was a child, although I was much healthier, I still experienced a lot of rejection from my peers. *Why?* I think the main reason is that my anomalies are tied to food. I can't eat many things most people can. Children didn't understand this so they chose to isolate me. In middle school, my peers slightly understood what a food allergy was, but since they hadn't heard of my allergies they became confused and would ostracize me. In high school, this trend continued, but there were a select few who chose to look past my allergies and not let them impede a friendship. There were still times when I wasn't invited to dinners or restaurants, and I was usually given this reason: "Well we didn't think there was anything you could eat, so we didn't invite you." I always tried to stress that the food wasn't important to me. For me, what mattered most was being with the people. Some understood, but others still couldn't grasp the concept. This trend continued even in college and sometimes with close friends. Nevertheless, there were still those priceless few who engaged me in whatever the activity was because they understood companionship was what I desired.

Only my family knows all the facets of my disease. If I told friends, it would confuse them and potentially drive them away. Therefore, I usually don't talk about what my body goes through unless they ask or I see in their eyes they want the full truth. Let's just say I have three groups of good friends:

My first group of friends cope with my disease by pretending it doesn't exist. They know I'm different and they know I'm sick, but they leave it at that. They accept the health regime I have to follow, but usually don't ask for

details or even about my health.
I'm fine with that. They are still
good friends, even if my health
may be a taboo subject to discuss.

Other friends ask how I'm doing,
but in a hurried way. They don't
really want to know the answer or
spend time talking about my
health. I pick up on this fact and
usually tell them I'm fine or that
there isn't any news. They'll look
sad for a second and then move to
a "safer topic."

My third group of friends will ask
how I'm doing and really want to
know how I truly am. At times they
become frustrated because they
feel helpless. They deeply want to
change my situation. I tell those
friends, I'm not expecting them to
discover the miracle cure, I only
want their support and that does
more to help me than they know.
These friends have started to learn
that while they can't do anything to
fix the healthy issue, I need them
to remain close to me through it all

so that I can find strength to continue fighting.

Then there is my family. They are in a category of their own for they have traveled with me on this road the most. They aren't always on my road, but they join me the majority of the time. They have seen me at my worst and my best. They are fully aware of the anomalies and ambiguity that encompass my disease, but they don't run away. They know more details than they desire to know about my disease, but still haven't abandoned me. Even when they aren't on my road they talk to me from their road, encouraging me to not give up on my journey. They know I have my Guide, but they also know if I didn't have them, I'd ask my Guide to lead me Home. My family isn't ready for me to go Home yet and with them by my side, I've vowed to travel on my road a little longer.

Yes, all my life I've been different. There was never a point when I was "normal" and then became sick. However, my "normal" has changed numerous times as my health declined. Each time, though, I have learned how to adjust. Hence, I will continue adjusting because this is how I survive.

Dare to be Honest

March 25, 2014

Round and round they tumble. Disheartening, depressing, discouraging. Clanging into each other. Causing a raucous. Ominous. Enlarging and growing. Pressing down the hope and courage. Killing the drive to keep trying. An endless stream, rough and powerful. They haunt me. Distract me. Overwhelm me. There is no escaping them. For they reside in my brain. They are thoughts making even the sunniest days seem cloudy. Thoughts leaving me empty, sad, and alone. Thoughts that leave me wondering why I still try. Thoughts attempting to convince me it's not worth fighting anymore. Thoughts urging me to give up. Thoughts telling me lies. They scream at me. Echoing through my brain.

"You don't really fit in because your body doesn't work right."

"People distance themselves because they are scared of what may happen to you."

"Everyone thinks you're so strange because you can't drink or eat or do the things they can."

"You're alone."

"You'll never have a normal life."

"You've failed."

"You'll never get a job."

"You're not going to make it far in life."

"No one will ever figure out how to fix you."

"It's probably just an eating disorder like everyone else assumes."

"You really think someone would want to date you or even marry you? They'd have to commit to you and your illness."

Over and over these thoughts turn, bringing me low. They cause sadness and despair to seep into my emotions. Those thoughts have been at it for years. I couldn't tell you how long, but for as long as I can remember. I've tried to hide them, not admit them, and not acknowledge them. I've kept them buried deep in the recesses of my brain, trying to cover them up so no one else can see them. I don't want to be vulnerable. I don't want others to see those thoughts are there.

Buried emotions and thoughts are dangerous and damaging. I'm learning this, but it's hard. I've realized that hiding my thoughts isn't healthy so I'm starting to share some of them. I've opened up to my parents. I call them crying because I know if I continue to bury the emotions they'll just continue to build. My parents talk to me. Love me. Encourage me. Pray for me.

The thoughts, I shared with them, confused them. They asked if I they are a result of my health continuing to decline. They asked if this mental pain was as bad as the mental pain I experienced two years ago (July 2012), when I weighed more. I told them no. Two years ago, when I was at a healthy weight, those same thoughts, mentioned above, were still there. In addition to those thoughts there was excruciating pain, intense bloating, and sickening nausea. As a result it was worse back then. They asked me why I never said anything two years ago. Why I didn't speak up and tell someone. I know you're probably wondering the same thing.

I did try to say something, but everyone I talked to said that it was a phase I needed to get through. Things would get better as time passed and my physical symptoms would eventually resolve. So I stayed silent. I didn't want to keep bringing up the same topic since I felt those I talked to would only shut me down. I told myself, *Stay quiet and get it together. They are right, it'll get better with time*.

I buried my feelings instead of uncovering them. I sealed them instead of opening up to others. I shouldn't have listened to what the psychologist told me. He told me to bury these thoughts. He told me it would get better and I needed to change my thinking pattern. I needed to stop worrying about my emotions or certain feelings. Instead, I should focus on eating and taking care of myself. He told me I shouldn't bring up the subject again and no one could change those things, so I needed to learn to deal with it. From that moment, I buried these thoughts, even though I should've opened up to my parents, but I didn't. I tried to handle it alone. I didn't talk to anyone except God about it. He's been the only One I've truly been open with, until now.

I've always been hesitant to share my feelings. I've never really liked to and still don't like to. I hate that my feelings make me look weak. They make me feel vulnerable. I'm slowly learning though that, as I share, I actually become stronger and grow. Relief comes with sharing, and sometimes it feels as though a weight has been lifted off my shoulders.

My hesitation to open up also stems from having my trust broken on numerous occasions. Each time I vowed I'd never make that mistake again. That promise only caused me to hide deep within myself. I tried to shield myself. The shield did offer protection, but it also kept me from opening up to those who care. Those who wouldn't break my trust.

How have I handled the thoughts and stress alone? Well, I haven't been alone. I've talked to Jesus. I've had Him to lean on. Honestly, that's probably the only way I've coped with the inward turmoil. I know those thoughts are lies, planted by the scheming devil. I know he seeks to pull me from my Savior's arms. I recognize that if I let my emotions overtake me I'd allow Satan to win, and in my playbook that's a very dangerous move that could cost me the game. I'm a victor because I've prayed to Jesus, asking Him to hold me, to shelter me, to protect me. And He has. He has let a song play at just the right time. He's soothed me with His promises. He's comforted me His Word. This is how I've dealt with the feelings.

Yet, He has nudged me to open up, and not let my feelings stay buried. I needed to trust my parents so I could receive additional support from them. This semester I slowly opened up. It's scary at times because I don't want them to know how I'm feeling. I don't want to hurt them with my emotions, but I need to stop trying to protect them because I damage myself in the long run.

As a result, I began to tell them more about my mental battle two years ago. I told them my fears of being readmitted into the hospital. I don't want doctors treating me like I have an eating disorder. I told them I try to eat every day, but it's hard because I'm tired of the eating and vomiting cycle. However, even though the vomiting isn't good it's difficult whenever I don't vomit because I'm in agony for hours. I've shared my fears of sounding bulimic. You see I'm glad when the vomiting happens because I start to feel better. Nevertheless, I'm scared that subconsciously my body rejects the food as a protection mechanism trying to avoid the pain, nausea and fullness that occur otherwise. I told them about the thoughts in my brain that have been lurking there for years, but unfortunately I've never had the courage to talk address them. I think it's a lot for my parents to take in, but they've handled it graciously. Loving and supporting me all the more.

Some days are better and I feel happy and full of life. Other days are gloomy and I flounder in the flood of my emotions. Yet, I haven't drowned because Jesus is holding me tight. The devil tugs, but he is no match for my Savior.

Now I'm sharing with you because I want to warn people against making the same mistakes. If you bury your emotions too deep and never let them out, they'll begin to rot and bring you more misery. You may roll your eyes thinking that's the same speech you've heard before. That you don't need to open up and can handle it. I'm telling you from personal experience, you're lying to yourself. How do I know this? Well, I told myself the same lie. Dare to be honest. Find someone you can share your pain and sorrow with. Don't let it consume you.

It was difficult writing these thoughts down. Admitting to you what I feel is hard, but in a way I also feel relief. I decided to step out from behind my shield, just an inch so I could be honest with you. I hope through sharing my deepest feelings, you have the courage to dig up some of your painful emotions and share them with another, so you don't have to carry the burden alone.

Family and Friends

The Gift

May 25, 2014

"Is it time to signal the oxytocin to release in this woman so that her contractions can begin and she can give birth, my Lord?" the angel asked God.

"I have one more gift to bestow on the baby and then you may signal the oxytocin to release," replied the Father of the Universe.

"What gift is that?" Queried the angel.

"It's a gift I've meticulously crafted especially for this little baby girl, but it will not be perceived as a gift at first. Actually it will only be seen as a gift if the girl lets Me work in her life and use the gift for My glory," said Jehovah.

"You've always have been the type to give each baby you create a gift, but the gift only becomes apparent when the little one grows up and lets You use them for your glory. However, those who refuse to turn to You either never discover the gift You left for them or the gift appears as a curse to them. It would be easier if everyone let You use them, so they could discover what You've gifted them with," mused the angel.

"Yes, the people of this world would be much better off if they let Me use them for my glory, for so many gifts stay hidden and countless others are perceived as curses from Me. Nevertheless, I have vowed to give each and every person the freedom to choose Me, even though, at times, I want to shake some sense into them. Hence, I let them be until they choose Me, for I already chose them before they took their first breath. Simply choosing Me doesn't reveal the gift. They must also submit to Me and decide to let Me use them for My glory. It is then and only then when my gifts become apparent. Yet, some still refuse to let Me use them fully and it pains me each and every time this happens. I wish they understood how wide, how long, how high and how deep my love is for them (Ephesians 3:18, NIV)," said God with a hint of sorrow in His voice.

"At least there are those who do see, my Lord. I'm still interested in the gift for this baby girl, what are You giving her?" questioned the angel.

"As I knit together this baby's digestive system I wove an extra component into it that I have never woven into anyone else," replied God.

"Have you given her the ability to digest anything?" inquired the angel.

God chuckled as He envisioned someone with that capability. "No, quite the contrary. I've woven a component into her digestive system that will make digestion extremely slow and difficult. It will cause her problems from her infancy, but I will not let it unleash its full potency until she is older. Around the time she starts high school, I will cause it to make its first harsh appearance. After many agonizing months, it will seem as if they fixed the problem and then everything will go back to normal. However four years later, after her freshman year of college, I will make it appear with even greater potency than before. It will tear her apart—physically, emotionally, psychologically, and spiritually. She'll fight a giant battle. Yet, I will surround her with a support system—starting with her family and branching out to countless others, for she will need the support in order to survive. Come to think of it, if I don't provide the support system, she won't survive it, because nothing will be motivate her to stay on the earth. She will think it's better to stop fighting and come home to Me in Heaven. For she'll know in Heaven there will be no pain or suffering. Then she'd finally be free of her torment."

"Will she pull through or will she come here?" asked the angel.

"She will pull through, but she will have to miss a full year of college, because of it," God answered.

"So she'll fall behind in school then?" reasoned the angel.

"Many will tell her she will never graduate on time. Others will convince her that graduating with her friends will be impossible and she should go easy on her course schedule, graduating in five or six years, instead of four. However, I've instilled a stubborn spirit in her and if she asks for My help, I will give her the strength and resolve necessary to balance her health and school, hence making it possible for her to graduate with

those she started with," God said
with a twinkle in His eye.

"So she'll be completely better
when she returns to school after
the year she misses?" probed the
angel.

"I suppose that would be nice if
that happened, but I have a bigger
plan for her. It will seem as though
she is better because she'll be at a
healthy weight and she will be
eating like a normal person.
Truthfully to most it will seem as if
her symptoms will be gone and she
is 100 percent normal, but that
won't be the case. One of this girl's
weaknesses will be her ability to
hide her internal emotions. Even
when she's in pain or hurting it will
be difficult for others to tell
because she will be extremely
skilled at hiding it. She'll become
so skilled she can even hide it from
her own family. Nevertheless, I will
give the girl's mother the ability to
see through the mask ninety-seven
percent of the time, because this

girl will need someone who can see beyond the mask. I will gift her father with the same ability, but her mother's nursing background will give her an advantage over her father," explained God.

"Okay but I'm confused. Will the girl be better when she goes back to school?" asked the perplexed angel.

"She will appear to be better, even to her own family, but on the inside she will hide a secret. The secret that there is still extreme pain, nausea, and bloating when she eats. Those feelings, after each meal, will throw her mind and body into chaos and the only thing she'll want to do, at that point, is to get rid of the food causing her so much agony. Eventually, she will share this with her mother, but it will not be until the girl has dealt with it for many months. This news will cause the mother great pain, however, because she thought her precious daughter was finally better. Yet, the mother will not give up on her daughter and she will try to find some solution to the problem," said God with a knowing look in His eyes.

"But Lord," questioned the angel, "What happens to the girl, will she graduate?"

"Yes, the girl will graduate with the peers she started with. She won't be held back, but only because she calls on My name for help. I will orchestrate the timing of so many things, she will know, without a shadow of a doubt, My perfect timing allowed this to happen. She will learn she can't go a single day without My strength infusing her. She will learn to block out the lies many tell her and listen for My voice of truth. She will learn the only reason she is still alive is because I carry her through the hardest times of her life. She will acknowledge the reason she was able to accomplish so much is because I guided her through it all."

"Nevertheless, she will still be plagued by her digestive system. The last two years of her undergraduate career will be full of doctor appointments, which take her all over the country. No solutions will be found. She'll be able to eat, but when she does eat she'll vomit ninety-nine percent of the time. The only times she won't vomit will be when she eats very small amounts. Mental anguish will plague her because she'll want to eat normally, but it won't be possible."

"She'll enjoy the food she eats and she'll eat meals, but her body will always be thrown into physical anguish after each meal. The pain will tear away at her, she'll vomit and eventually feel better, but that pattern of eat→pain→vomit→repeat will wear away at her. It will confuse and frustrate her. She'll be angry at her body for not working right and for rejecting the food she tries to put in it. She'll be frustrated she can't eat without being in agony. She'll be annoyed each time after she eats a meal, because she will become grumpy and snappy as a result of the pain and discomfort, which put her on edge. She'll become exasperated there isn't relief without vomiting. She won't make herself vomit, but she will feel guilty about the fact that sometimes she wants to vomit so she can feel better. She'll feel guilty because of the bulimia stereotype associated with vomiting and she will fear being labeled with this stereotype."

"She'll know deep down that she is sicker than she ever was in the past, but she'll resist another hospitalization. She'll resist it because she doesn't want to spend more months in a hospital regaining weight without actually fixing the problem. She will near exhaustion. She'll feel like she can't go on. She'll debate whether the daily battle with her symptoms is worth fighting. Yet in the end she'll keep fighting because I will make sure she's surrounded by those who love her," said God with a pained look in His eyes.

"Father, there is pain in Your eyes as You speak, why? And forgive me if I'm missing this, but I'm confused about how all of what You just said is a gift for the girl? How can all that pain and suffering be a gift? Won't she see it as a punishment from You? Won't she hate You for it? Won't she be angry at You?" queried the angel.

"My faithful servant, there is pain in my eyes because I know the suffering this girl will endure and I never wish for any of my children to suffer. Nevertheless, it must come to pass so that through the suffering she can touch others. For I've already ingrained in this baby girl's brain the intense desire to help all those who suffer. Her heart will break each time she sees anything I have created suffering. From the tiny field mouse to a full-grown human, when she sees someone or something in anguish her desire will be to bring them relief."

"She'll have the option of becoming angry with Me and hating Me for giving her the disease. She will cry out to Me daily and beg Me to give her strength to fight another day. However, she'll also implore I use the sickness that ravages her body, to bring glory to My name. She'll ask Me to turn all the bad of her disease into good for others. She'll view her illness as the gift I intended it to be. Not a gift necessarily for her, but something she can turn into a gift for others. Through her disease, she will gain a clearer understanding of what suffering entails. She will learn what it's like to endure nights without sleep because the pain prevents rest from coming. She will better understand what it's like to deal with a condition that remains undiagnosed and how to stay strong through uncertainty. She will discover what it feels like to be subjected to test after test in the hospital and what it's like to live in the hospital for a long period of time."

"She will learn all of this and a great deal more. This knowledge will allow her to connect with people she never would've otherwise. If she continues to trust Me, I will show her how she can use the gift I've given her, to touch many people. However, she must rely on Me and trust in Me, for Satan will hover nearby, ready to pounce if she starts to turn from Me. Whenever the devil is near enough to whisper in her ear, he will try to convince her to become angry with me. He wants her to see My gift as a curse and to give up in her fight, but as long as she looks to Me, I will give her the strength to resist his lies. She will find victory in Me," said God as a gentle smile played at His lips."

"I think I'm beginning to see how the disease is a gift, but it only can be a gift if she chooses to let You use her," pondered the angel. "What happens after she graduates from college and finishes her undergraduate career? Will she go to graduate school? What about her disease, will they find a cure? Will she get married and have a family of her own?"

"I have already revealed to you how the first twenty-two years of this baby girl's life will progress, in order to show you how my gift would play out at the start. Now that you understand how My gift will work, I'll let you discover, on your own, how the rest of her life will play out."

"Now, go, signal the oxytocin to release in the mother so in a few hours this baby girl will be born. I am also giving you the task of watching over this girl as she grows. You may let her foot slip at times, but never let her fall unless she no longer wants Me in her life. Guard her well my servant for the devil will wage more and more attacks on her as she grows because he will want to convince her to abandon Me. He will try to convince her to give up her fight against this disease. Guard her well and fight off the demons when she calls out for help. She can't do it in her own strength and when she recognizes that, go to her aid."

"When she seems low and wants to be home with Me, remind her, I will call her home when the time is right. I need her to press on for a little longer so she can touch more lives. Let her know I'm fully aware of her suffering and it breaks my heart, but I need her to endure it a little longer. Remind her I will bring her home to a place with no pain or suffering, someday soon, and Heaven will seem much sweeter because of what she endured on the earth. Never let her forget that she is My child and that I love her deeply! Now, go my angel; I have given you a special task, do not fail Me," commanded God.

"I'm honored by You giving me this baby girl to watch over and protect as she grows. I will not fail you, my Lord," vowed the angel. He then flew out from God's presence down to earth, to the little town of Pax River, Maryland. There he found the mother and he signaled the oxytocin to be released.

Hours later, on the evening of May 18, 1992, the mother held the baby girl in her arms. The tired mother kissed the baby girl on her head and whispered a promise "I love you so much and always will my beautiful baby girl. Kristen Elizabeth Fox you are my daughter and I will fight for you and support you throughout your life."

The angel murmured softly, "Your daughter has a tough road ahead of her and you keeping that promise will be one of the major reasons she makes it as far as she does. May God the Father infuse strength into you and your husband for the journey that is to come."

The Tattoo

February 15, 2014

The pen etched a line of fire along my slender ankle. I gripped the outstretched hand of the handsome lad sitting next to me. My face remained blank; I refused to let the pain I felt become visible to those around me.

The boy turned to me and said, "It's hurting you, isn't it?"

I let a small laugh escape my mouth as I said, "You know me so well that you see the pain I try to hide."

He simply nodded, but I read the message within the nod. Very few people know when I'm in pain, but my family has learned to read my eyes, the one part of my face I have never figured out how to mask. My brother was no exception. This time, however, the source of my pain was not because of my illness. This time I'd willingly agreed to the pain because it was merely a means to an end. An end that would be a symbol, a reminder and a motivator for me as I continue fighting my battle.

I looked down to the device creating the fiery line around my ankle. The black tattoo gun, holding nine microscopic needles, made a soft buzzing noise. The tattoo artist, who deftly held the gun, focused on his masterpiece and paid attention to every detail.

Almost two years ago, I sat on my stark white hospital bed, engrossed in the hedgehog cross-stich I'd worked on the last few days. My head came up as I heard a knock on the door. A hospital volunteer stuck her head in the door and asked if I wanted a gift canister. I smiled and agreed. She handed me a plastic jar and then left the room. The jar contained knick-knacks, a Winnie the Pooh puzzle, plastic figurines and a blue rubber bracelet inscribed with *Never Give Up* (much like the yellow *Livestrong*® bracelets that circulated a few years ago). I slipped it around my ankle and vowed never to take it off, for it would be a constant reminder to keep fighting.

A year and a half later, the bracelet was still on my ankle, but an idea had formed in my mind. I decided to tell my brother first, while we explored Colorado together. I told him instead of wearing a blue bracelet on my ankle for the rest of my life; I'd get the phrase "Never Give Up" tattooed on my ankle. The saying could then literally become a part of me. He liked the idea and during the summer of 2013 we visited various tattoo shops scattered throughout the city.

My parents took the news with grace but declined to give an opinion. They merely said they were glad this was something I'd thought through and not a whimsical decision. The price of a tattoo was more than I was willing to pay at the time, so I left for college, that fall, still wearing the blue bracelet.

One evening, during the middle of my fall semester my brother and I were talking online and he sent me a website link for a shirt he wanted for Christmas. I told him I'd look into it and jokingly reminded him that he forgot a present for my twenty-first birthday. He told me he actually wanted to combine my twenty-first birthday plus Christmas gift and pay for the tattoo I wanted. I was shocked. I couldn't believe what he had told me. Excitement surged through my body as I realized something I'd merely dreamed of would soon be a reality.

When I came home for winter break, I called a tattoo shop my brother found and requested the artist he had researched. They worked me in on November 19, 2013 at noon. I realized later that it was a near miracle that I got an appointment, since I had called only a week out. The 19th of the month held special significance for me because it fell between the 18th and 20th of the month. The 18th marks the day of the month I was born on and the 20th marks the day of the month my brother was born on.

My brother said he'd take me to the appointment, sit with me, and support me. However, he got scheduled to work that morning. Instead of working, he called around to fellow co-workers to cover his shift. He never had, in his history of working, asked for someone to cover his shift and he has yet to do it again.

I came up with a plan for my tattoo and finalized it with my brother. We decided on a Bible passage reference, we both enjoyed, to incorporate into the tattoo. The bible passage we picked was Psalm 139, for each part of this verse holds a message of hope and peace, which are detailed below. *Note: A few months later, my brother got the same reference incorporated into a tattoo of his own. Thus we will forever share that link.*

Psalm 139 (NIV)

1 O LORD, you have searched me and you know me. 2 You know when I sit and when I rise; you perceive my thoughts from afar. 3 You discern my going out and my lying down; you are familiar with all my ways. 4 Before a word is on my tongue you know it completely, O LORD. 5 You hem me in-- behind and before; you have laid your hand upon me. 6 Such knowledge is too wonderful for me, too lofty for me to attain. *God always watches over me. His presence surrounds me even when* *trouble ensnares me, He makes sure I can make it through. He knows what I'm thinking, even before the thoughts enter my head. He knows when I'm scared, anxious, and afraid, even before I begin to feel those emotions. Although I may be able to mask my emotions from those around me, I can never mask them from Him. He knows everything before it happens, He's ready with a plan to help me through each obstacle I'll encounter, long before I ever encounter it.*

7 Where can I go from your Spirit? Where can I flee from your presence? 8 If I go up to the heavens, you are there; if I make my bed in the depths, you are there. *As long as I can remember, I've never tried to flee from God. There have been numerous times when I've sinned and disappointed Him, but I don't think I've ever tried to flee from Him because, in reality, it's impossible. God always knows* *where you're at and it's impossible to hide from Him. If God were to play the game hide-and-seek, He'd know exactly where you were before He finished counting to ten.*

9 If I rise on the wings of the dawn, if I settle on the far side of the sea, 10 even there your hand will guide me, your right hand will hold me fast. *As I look over my life, especially the past few years, the poem,"Footprints[1]" comes to mind. This famous poem is about a man looking over his life with Jesus. Many times he sees two sets of footprints in the sand, his set and Jesus' set. However, he notices that during the hardest times in his life, there was only one set of footprints in the sand. He looked at Jesus and asked Him why He abandoned him during the worst moments of His life. With eyes full of love, Jesus turned to the man and told him, "My child, I would never leave you. When you see one set of footprints in the sand, it was then that I carried* *you." I know if I were to look at the path my life has traced in the sand, I would only see one set of footprints, for Jesus has carried me.*

11 **If I say, "Surely the darkness will hide me and the light become night around me," 12 even the darkness will not be dark to you; the night will shine like the day, for darkness is as light to you."** *During the course of my disease, I have felt as though a darkness surrounds me. As though I'm stuck somewhere no light can enter. Yet the darkness holds no meaning to God. The darkness may overwhelm me and I may feel as though no one can see me because it enshrouds my entire being, but to God, the darkness is as light as day and He can see his precious child from a mile away. Therefore I can rest easy knowing no matter how dark my life may seem, God is still beside me and I'll never be hard for Him to see.*

13 For you created my inmost being; you knit me together in my mother's womb. 14 I praise you because I am fearfully and wonderfully made; your works are wonderful, I know that full well. 15 My frame was not hidden from you when I was made in the secret place. When I was woven together in the depths of the earth, 16 your eyes saw my unformed body. All the days ordained for me were written in your book before one of them came to be.

I was born with a gastrointestinal motility problem, which becomes worse with each passing year, but I was no mistake. God created each of the molecules that comprise my body. He made my digestive system and because of that, no matter the pain or sickness that consumes, I am fearfully and wonderfully made. For God's masterpieces aren't flawed. He does not make errors in His designs. Therefore, I'm not broken, a mistake or flawed. I may not have a perfect body or a perfect life, and I may be fighting for the life God gave me, but He gave me this disease for a reason. It may cause difficult circumstances in my life, but I want to turn those into opportunities to touch, help, and impact others through my suffering. God gave me this for a reason, shame on me, if I waste that gift and don't use it to make an impact on those whom He puts into my life.

17 How precious to me are your thoughts, O God! How vast is the sum of them! 18 Were I to count them, they would outnumber the grains of sand. When I awake, I am still with you. *God is the greatest philosopher out there. His thoughts are more precious than the combined thoughts of Einstein, Aristotle, and Socrates. His wisdom is more infinite than anyone else. He sees the big picture. A picture I rarely see and thus I need to trust His perfect plan. Therefore, I pray*

*that His Spirit, not a spirit of fear
or anxiety, will consume me
concerning the future.*

**18 (cont.) When I awake, I am
still with you.** *There are times
when I'm scared to fall asleep
because I feel sick and have
intense pain. I'm afraid if I fall
asleep I won't wake up again. Yet,
God is with me when I fear and He
wakes me up each morning. Even
if I didn't wake up, it wouldn't
signify that He left me, rather I'd
be in His very presence.*

**19 If only you would slay the
wicked, O God! Away from me,
you bloodthirsty men! 20 They
speak of you with evil intent;
your adversaries misuse your
name. 21 Do I not hate those
who hate you, O LORD, and
abhor those who rise up
against you? 22 I have nothing
but hatred for them; I count
them my enemies.** *These verses
remind me that when others tell
me I'm ugly or too skinny, I should*

pay them no mind, for they speak contrary to what God says. When troubles arise in the world, like terrorist attacks, murder or any other tragedy, I can feel safe because God doesn't support their evil ways. If God is for us, who can be against us?" (Romans 8:31, NIV).

23 Search me, O God, and know my heart; test me and know my anxious thoughts. 24 See if there is any offensive way in me, and lead me in the way everlasting. *Psalm 139 ends with these two verses. They remind me to pray and ask God for guidance in my life. They also remind me to ask God for forgiveness when I've wronged Him. They encourage me to keep my heart pure and true; to obey His teachings; to love all. They challenge me to serve and sacrifice for others, just as God sacrificed his Son so one day I could spend eternity in Heaven with my Savior. What a day that will be! I'll no longer endure the* *agony, torture or sickness I experience on a daily basis. I'm by no means perfect. I don't love everyone or treat everyone like Jesus would. I'm not willing to help all that I meet, but I try each day to follow Jesus' example. I can't in my own strength, but Psalm 139 reminds me where my strength comes from. Even though I struggle, His hand firmly grasps mine so I'll never be out of His reach.*

Another element to my tattoo is an arrow. The fletching (feathers) of the arrow stick out from the "P" of Psalm and the head of the arrow protrudes from the nine of "139." The arrow was one of the earliest weapons. It has been around for centuries and is symbolic. It reminds me to fly straight and true in my journey. It's a quiet but deadly weapon and it reminds me that sometimes quiet weapons, like love, are more effective, than those weapons that create noise, like hate. It takes great skill and practice to shoot an arrow and hit the center of the target, so it reminds me to do everything with excellence and skill. Perseverance can reap great benefits. Lastly, it challenges me to live life seeking to reach the goals (or targets) before me.

Finally, and probably most significant, is the phrase "Never Give Up" etched in flowing script around the rest of my ankle. Nestled in the phrase are the first initials of each member of my family. I don't fight for myself, but for those I love and care about, because I don't want them to suffer from losing me. So I decided to incorporate my family into my tattoo, as a reminder of why I press on. Along the left-hand side of the "N" for "Never," "FOX" is etched into my skin, for we're connected by our last name. On the right-hand side of the "N" is a "T" is woven into the script for my daddy, Tim. Incorporated in the "G" for "Give" is a "C" for my mommy, Cynthia. Finally intertwined with the "U" for "Up," is a "K" for my little brother, Kevin. My family has been my greatest support and they are the main reason I vow to "Never Give Up!"

The color of the tattoo is black, but shaded in the words of "Never Give Up" is a muted royal blue. The color blue symbolizes peace, healing, and serenity. Plus blue has been my favorite color since I was a child. Furthermore, blue is a symbol of water. Water is a vital source for our survival. Without it we'd die. Not only do I drink water regularly, but Jesus also gives me His living water to drink, which daily strengthens me. His water is in the form of His Word, the Bible, and the people He put in my life to encourage and comfort me. Finally royal blue is one of the school colors for University of Florida!

Even the placement of my tattoo has significance. It is around my left ankle. I have always been left-side dominant. Side Note: Left-side dominance is much less common than right-side dominance. Furthermore, my feeding tube is located on the left side of my abdomen. Finally, I've always enjoyed running and sadly I haven't been able to run these last three years. Your ankles are a key player for running since your ankle joint is where your foot attaches to your leg. I continue to fight so one day I can run again. My dream is to run the Around the World Disney Marathon®, so we'll see if that goal can be accomplished someday.

I don't think this tattoo will be something I regret. It's something special I share with my little brother. It reminds me why I fight and about the God who watches over me. The day I got my tattoo was the first time I had removed the blue bracelet in almost two years. I decided to give that bracelet to my brother, since he was the one who gave me my tattoo.

My tattoo wasn't a sign of defiance or trying to be hip. My tattoo holds a story and has symbolism. It represents my battle, my faith, and my family, and is a continuous reminder to Never Give Up.

The Tattoo

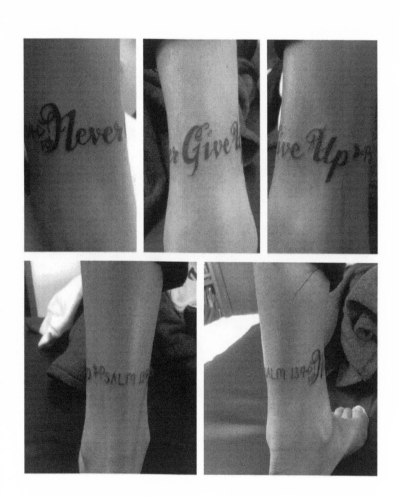

Family

June 18, 2014

His heart broke as he watched one
of his most prized possessions
waste away. He had made a
promise more than twenty-two
years ago to protect, guard, and
nurture her, yet he could do
nothing to ease the torment
draining the life from her body.
When God gave him his little
princess he had promised he'd go
so far as to give up his life for her,
if it meant she could be saved, but
there was nothing he could do to
stop her torture. He would gladly
bear her burden if it meant the
pain no longer resided in her eyes.

She bore the suffering well,
disguising it from most, but as her
father, he could tell she was far
from okay. He could read the signs
no one else could because he was
her daddy, and though she tried,
she couldn't completely disguise
her suffering from him. The only

thing left for him to do was to pray, and he prayed daily for her. His knees were worn from the hours he spent on them, crying out to his heavenly Father to ease her suffering. The other thing he could do was pour out his love and support. This let her know she wasn't alone and he would stick by her side until either he was taken from this earth or she was called home.

A mother's job was to kiss an "owie" and for it to go away. Yet, for twenty-two years, even though she'd kissed her daughter numerous times, the "owie" never went away. The mother's heart broke daily as she watched her once vibrant daughter tire from climbing a staircase. It seemed as though her daughter's ghost roamed the house because the girl before her was simply a shadow of her former self. The youth and vitality were stripped from her body. Her clothes hung loosely on her frame and when she wore shorts or short-sleeved shirts, her limbs looked like thin twigs poking from the gaping holes. Pain clouded her eyes and her spirit was much quieter than it had been.

The mother's occupation was as a nurse and because of this she experienced an even greater level of frustration. No mother wants to see their child suffer and be powerless to stop the suffering. However, a nurse who is also a mom has an even greater struggle witnessing this. The only thing left this mother could do was beg her Savior to restore her daughter's health. In the meantime, she would comfort and support her daughter as best she could. She would dry any tears that fell, hold her little girl's fragile hand as she underwent numerous tests and advocate for her daughter when doctors pushed her around. She wouldn't give up on her daughter, even if her daughter chose to give up on herself.

The loyalty and love he held for his sister was deeper than any he held for any other. She was his big sister, the person he'd always looked up to and the one he always feared losing. He had once said to her he'd overcome all of his fears, except the fear of losing her. He didn't like being at hospitals, but if she was there he always went. It didn't matter where his big sister was, if she needed him, he'd be there. He never tried to hide his sister from his friends, even though her skeleton frame and sickly appearance brought on a barrage of questions from them. He always invited her to do things with him and his friends because he knew she'd enjoy the diversion. It didn't matter to him what she looked like; he loved her all the same. He wished he could do something to help her pain, but since he couldn't, he prayed for her and supported and loved her.

I know I've talked about my family time and time again, but I could never mention them too much. Why? Their love and support are what keeps me going. Even when I've yelled at them to leave me alone, I've never truly meant it. For on the inside, I'm begging them to stay. Even at twenty-two years of age and a college graduate, when I'm at an age where I'm expected to do things on my own, my parents make sure to let me know they don't consider their job as parents over. They also make sure to clear their work schedules if I have a doctor appointment, so I don't have to go alone. At times, my mom doesn't even come into the appointment with me, instead she'll stay in the waiting room, but she is ready to be an advocate for me, if I need one. That's extremely comforting for me to know.

Another common trend for college graduates is to move out of their parents' home and start a job and life of their own. However, my parents made it clear to me, I'm welcome to live with them and I had a place in their home until I was healthy enough to start a life of my own. If I had to worry about finding a full-time job so I could pay for a place to live and my medical expenses, I'd likely be dead by now. I'm in no shape to do that. Yet, I'm not dead because I have a family who's committed to me.

A lot of people wonder what they can do when their family member, close friend or acquaintance becomes sick. People never know what to say or what they can do to help so they do nothing or avoid contact with him or her. One of the hardest things I've dealt with throughout my disease is people walking out of my life because they didn't think they could do anything to help me. They feared what they'd see happen to me, if they kept being my friend. If someone you know becomes sick, don't immediately freak out and cut ties with them because that won't help him or her with what's happening. You don't need to do much, saying hi and asking how life's been can enough to brighten his or her day.

For those of you already invested in the sick person (maybe he or she is family or a close friend) there isn't much you can do to ease the pain. Instead, be there for them. Let them know you won't desert them. I know I treasure every letter and care package I receive. Getting a care package brightens my day in ways no one can understand. It doesn't even have to be something big, but something as simple as a note or a movie or some tea can bolster my spirit in ways people don't understand. Furthermore, even something as "little" as a Facebook message, email, etc. can go leaps and bounds in improving my mood for the day.

I've realized those who feel the most helpless (friends or relatives) can actually do the most to encourage me by letting me know they are thinking of me. It goes to show, you don't need to find the cure or invent a new technology in order to help the hurting person in your life. Most people just want someone to show they care. Even those sick people, who act like they don't want anyone around, really do want someone to show them they care. Next time you hear your friend is sick or even if it's your own brother, remember you can do so much to help them by letting them know you're there.

Another thing I've noticed is when an illness is chronic or requires long-term treatment, many start to think another card or another text will be repetitive and annoying. Well, that is a big fat lie. When the treatment is long-term or the disease chronic, life is more difficult. At least with an acute illness, a person is better within weeks or months, but with a chronic illness or treatment, you aren't better in a short amount of time. After several months have passed the journey becomes even more difficult because you begin to wonder why you bother to fight. At this point, the support from others is even more crucial. Again, it doesn't have to be anything big, but a simple text can make anyone's day a lot brighter and simultaneously give them strength and hope to keep fighting.

I can say, without a doubt, people's texts, letters, care packages, etc. have done more for me than anything the doctors have done. I'm still here, for the doctors to do tests on, because so many have shown me support and love.

I've also noticed, people don't always know how to act around me. It's almost as if they wonder if our conversations need to be serious because of everything happening to me. My answer is no! My closest friends treat me like I want to be treated. I strive to live my life as normal as possible, so it helps when people treat me as a normal human being. The friends, who've joked about my tube or backpack, have also been the friends who have been able to bolster me more than others. The person who is sick obviously knows he or she is sick. They know the situation is serious and also know their life isn't normal, but you don't need to remind them of that by treating them like they are really sick. Don't joke about something you think might offend the person. At the same time, don't treat him or her with such gravity. It helps when people don't treat me so seriously because it helps me feel normal, even though I know I'm not. I understand the gravity of my situation. I understand I'm at high risk for heart attack and stroke because my blood work shows abnormalities. I know that I'm in a critical state, but I don't need everyone treating me like that so I'm constantly reminded of it.

I guess this brings me full circle

because my family has grasped that I want to live my life as normally as possible, for as long as I can. They shower me with their love and support, but aren't constantly acknowledging everything going wrong with my body. They let me live at home, be alone, and go to friend's houses. We have conversations about the weather, the latest headline or what we're doing during the week. This normalcy helps me stay sane

Daddy's Girl

August 9, 2014

This essay is dedicated to Tim Fox, my daddy.

I will always be a daddy's girl. It's plain and simple as that. However, I wouldn't be a daddy's girl if it weren't for the man I have the privilege to call daddy. I always say I'll be lucky if I find a guy to marry who is just fifty percent of my dad. God blessed me when He gave me to this man.

From day one, my daddy has always treated me with respect, gentleness, and love. He has never tried to hide my presence, but has always made me feel special by showing me off. He has not only called me his princess, but treated me as one too. He has always taken time out to do special things for me. These memories are forever seared in my brain.

I remember a strong hand gently shaking me awake on numerous fishing season mornings. I'd groggily sit up in bed and would see my daddy squatting next to me whispering it was time to go. I'd get out of bed and climb into the old clothes my mommy had put out for me the night before. Then we were off. I'd sit proudly next to my daddy in his truck. On the way to the ocean, we'd always stop at this little bagel shop and I'd get a poppy seed bagel with cream cheese while my dad would order a sesame seed or plain bagel. Then we were off again, our next stop the ocean. When we arrived, we'd finish our bagels and then meander down to the shoreline. I'd promptly dig holes in the sand, down to the water line so the water would fill up my hole. Then I'd sit and wait for daddy to catch a fish. I'd help him put the bait on the hook because I had to make sure he didn't prick his finger. Then I'd watch him flawlessly cast his line. The nearly invisible string disappearing from my sight as it flew through the air. Soon my daddy would start reeling that baby in. Whenever he caught something we could keep, I'd put it in my premade holes so that the fish could swim around and breathe. We made a great team.

As I got older, my dad never stopped taking me out on dates. We would go to my favorite restaurant, the newest coffee shop, the merry-go-round, the movies or wherever my heart desired. Usually, it was my choice and if it wasn't, my dad always had a really good idea up his sleeve. The most exciting part about going to restaurants was that I didn't have to use the kid's menu, but I could order off the same menu that my daddy used.

My daddy promised me that he would guard my heart until he gave me away on my wedding day. Now many may scoff at the phrase "guard my heart." I once thought it was kind of silly and sadly it took me years to understand the gravity of that promise. He's saying he will do his best to protect me from any danger until another man is qualified enough for the job. A qualification my dad promised he would verify before giving me away. This is just another example of how my father makes sure I am protected and safe.

Therefore, imagine the pain my father goes through knowing he's unable to protect me from the thing that hurts me the most. Imagine the tears he has shed as he watches his little girl succumb to test after test, watching her writhe in pain and wiping hot tears from her cheeks. Yet, he has not taken on a spirit of defeat. No, he constantly works to make sure he is doing all in his power to help me, to be there for me and to show me love.

During my hospitalization in 2012, he came to visit me almost every day. One day, I was in such a bad mood I decided I wouldn't talk. Instead of leaving, he quietly sat by my bedside and did nothing else but sat there, letting his presence be known. Then a few hours later he scooted closer and began to stroke my hair. He said nothing, just massaged my head. Tears streamed down my face. I had been a jerk to him, but he didn't let that stop him from loving me. Instead, he patiently sat by my side so I would know I wasn't alone.

Even now, in my emaciated form, my daddy still reminds me I'm beautiful. Reminding me that beauty is not just about the outside, but also the inside. He supports me and always makes sure I realize he's there if I need something. I also know he prays for me on a daily basis. I can't imagine the prayers he's presented God with. I do know he's cried out in distress and anguish countless times, begging God to take this from me.

He always told me he wished he could take my disease from me and suffer from it instead. Ironically, one of my biggest praises is I suffer from the disease instead of him. It's mainly for selfish reasons because I don't know if I could stay strong enough to watch one of my family members go through this. People always say I'm so strong, but they fail to realize my family is much stronger because they've had to watch someone they love go through it versus having to go through it on their own.

My daddy is the man I first loved. He's my protector. My friend. My counselor. My advisor. He is my king. I am his princess.

Here are some poems I wrote to express my father's love and also the speech I gave at his retirement ceremony, which demonstrates the sacrifices my daddy has made so I can have him in my life.

Dad

On Father's Day this year
I want to make it clear
For all the world to see
How much my Dad means to me

For on this day last year
I had a lot of fear
It was when my first pain came
And from then I was never the
same

This year has held many trials
And we have traveled many miles
To figure out a fix
To get me outa this mix

And throughout this all
My Dad was there so I couldn't fall
He sacrificed so many hours
He brought me tons of flowers

His worry shown through his tears
To his God he cried out many
prayers

And all of this and more he did
Because I am his kid

I am so proud to call him Dad
Without him I'd be sad
So thank you to the man I love
For you've brought me hope, like
Noah's dove

Daddy's Girl

From the moment I was born
I stuck like a thorn
To the side of the man
Who would be my biggest fan
Gently he held me
Stroking my knee
Safe in his arms
All fears disarmed
He hands were so gentle
Yet calloused and so instrumental
His eyes held love so pure
His voice like liquid myrrh
Throughout the years those eyes
and voice
Would be a constant comfort and
my top choice
No matter the struggle

Even if there was trouble
Never did he falter
Always kneeling at the altar
Talking to his God
Because in his heart there would
be no fraud
Forever patient and kind
Keeping me at the front of his mind
Holding my hand
Guiding me through the sand
At times I would look back on our
travels
And I would see when I became
unraveled
But instead of abandonment
I would find he went
Knelt down
And carried me without a frown
Forever his little princess I would
be
No other man could take that from
me
Of course he will give me away one
day
But part of me will always be his to
stay
Even when gray hairs crown his
brow
He will be my King as he is now

Daddy's girl is my label
And trust me this is no fable
I wear it with pride
For its namesake is my wonderful
guide
Through life he will be mine
And with him by my side I can
shine

Father's Love

Quite and gentle
His voice brought calm
Through the nightmares
And the storms
His voice could always be heard
It was a comfort
Beyond all other
It was a sound
That put the weary mind to rest
It was the sound of a father's love

Callused and gentle
His hands brought love
As they rubbed and they held
The child
Safe and secure
Were the hands of his
For they could hold up mountains

And stop great rivers
So that the child would be safe
These were the hands of a loving
father

Bright and blue
Solemn and quite
The eyes that held great wisdom
The eyes that knew all things
The eyes that we gentle
The eyes that meant you were in
trouble
The eyes of a father with love

Tall and straight
Proud and great
Not thinking out for himself
Just looking out our health
Never complaining
Always campaigning
For our safety
And our security
This was the father's love

Doing things to make it better for
those he loved
Not overworking

But taking time
For the one's he loved
This was the father's love

Never selfish
Always giving
Looking forward
Never back
Pressing on
Keeping with it
Showing courage
Loving always
This was the father's love

Retirement Speech

Many of you know Tim Fox as a captain, a leader, and a friend. My beautiful mother has the honor of calling him husband. I take great pride in calling him my father. I've never known a man as courteous, courageous, and admirable as my father. I have many fond memories of my father's military career: from pinning awards to his uniform to breaking handmade Mexican cascarones (hollowed-out chicken eggs filled with confetti) on his head in congratulations. One of my fondest memories was when he allowed me to keep a baby squirrel I found at one his Change of Commands (military promotion ceremonies). I remember running out to find the baby squirrel I saw before going to the Change of Command. Upon finding it, I wrapped it in my shawl and went in search of my dad. I spotted him standing proud and tall amongst other dignitaries. Instead of waiting until he was alone, I rushed up to him, my eyes shining with excitement as I showed him my new pet. Instead of yelling or getting upset at me, he examined my find and told me I could take it home to care for it. Little did I know, I'd look back on that moment years later and realize the amazing patience and love my father showed me that day.

Many of us, including me, will never know how many sacrifices my father made during his military career. I know many of the sacrifices he has made have been for the benefit of his family. He has given up promotions in order to be there as a father and a husband for the family he loves. There are not words I can say to express just how thankful I am for him taking these measures in order to be there for us. Many ask me if I enjoyed living in a military family and I can say I have loved it. I've had the great privilege to live in countless states and visit those I haven't lived in. Furthermore, I've gone to see parts of the world many only dream to see. Moving around has allowed me to become a well-rounded person and grow in ways I never imagined. Living in a military family has been a great honor and privilege and I couldn't be more proud of the man who has given me this experience. Before I end, I want to read a poem in honor of my father.

Retirement

He started as a young man
Consistently saying "I can"
He had a military dream
To be a member of the Navy team

And after years of hard work
Performing duties in which he did
not shirk
He obtained his Navy wings
And they became one of his most
treasured things

He always stood proud and tall
Never letting his comrade fall
His sharp salute was an example to
all
He never faltered in answering his
country's call

His character is only measurable to
some
And to all he would say come
Because of this he quickly
advanced

This did not happen purely by chance

From ensign to captain he has come so far
He became a rising star
Throughout it all putting his family first
Making sure we wouldn't be put through the worst

He has led his family and his squadrons well
All problems and fears he would quell
Always humble in his demeanor
Giving God the credit to the core

But now the time has come
For him to stop going to and from
For today we honor him
This man many know as Tim

For twenty-seven long years have come to an end
And today they do send
My father, my leader, my hero to shore
For there he will stay forevermore

Mamma's World

August 9, 2014

This essay is dedicated to Cynthia Fox, my mommy.

Just as I've been blessed with a wonderful father, I'm also lucky to have an amazing mother. A woman who has sacrificed more for me than anyone else. A woman who hasn't left my side, no matter how difficult the journey has become. A woman who emits comfort and love. A woman who has had my back throughout my entire battle.

The day I was born she promised she'd be there for me and it's a promise she has kept. She sacrificed her dream of practicing nursing to stay at home and raise me and my brother. That sacrifice allowed me to be brought up by my mom and not anyone else.

As you all know, I've had stomach issues since I was born. What many of you don't realize is I saw my first gastrointestinal (stomach) doctor at eighteen months. I underwent my first round of testing then. My mom has taken me to hospitals since I was eighteen months old and she continues to accompany me now, even though I'm twenty-two. That means for more than twenty years my mother has patiently stood by my side during every appointment and hospitalization. Do you realize the amount of strength this woman possesses? She has had to watch her little girl poked and prodded. She has had to watch her child suffer through anguish, turmoil, and heartache. She has had to live a mother's worst nightmare, and she has lived it with amazing strength, perseverance, and dedication.

She has been my biggest advocate at the hospital. When doctors have bullied me, she has calmly told them their behavior is unacceptable. She has vouched for me when my character has been questioned. She has not let me be abused by the health system. She has critically questioned doctors about treatments they propose in order to ensure it's the best option. Without her, I'm not sure where I'd be, but I definitely wouldn't be in a good place.

This battle has worn down my mother. I can see the pain in her eyes when I tell her I'm still not doing well or that I'm still vomiting. I hear the desperation in her voice as she tries to come up with new solutions or suggestions. I hear the hope in her language when she talks about a new medication or method I can use to possibly get better. I can't imagine the burden she bears and the pain she goes through as she watches me fight for my life.

My mother (and father for that matter) have backed me up when I've repeatedly explained to the doctors that I don't have an eating disorder. Imagine the confusion and doubt my parents have felt when doctors tell them I have an eating disorder, while I'm on the other end saying I really don't have one. Nevertheless, they have believed me. They have helped me fight the doctors' labeling and have advocated on my behalf. If my parents didn't believe me, I would feel alone and lost. It's critical for me that they don't think I have an eating disorder because one of my biggest fears is being written-off as someone suffering from one.

More than anyone else, my mom has felt the brunt of my frustration and confusion associated with my disease. I know there are countless times when I've taken these feelings out on her. I've yelled at her, accused her of things, and gotten upset at her for the slightest offense. Regardless, she has still shown me love and never left me alone. She knew that during these times I desperately needed and wanted her to stay by

my side despite the fact I was
screaming at her to go away.

My mommy also makes a big effort
to do special things with me. From
weekend excursions to the beach
or "The Big Apple," to getting
pedicures or going to the
movies, my mother has made it a
priority to set aside time solely
devoted to being with me. She
makes sure I still feel normal and
experience normal things in life.

Encouraging me to push beyond
the pain and keep trying is
something my mom has done more
than anyone else. I know she has
convinced me to try things I never
would have because I was too
scared to. She has influenced me
to change things I did and go
beyond my comfort zone. I
probably wouldn't be alive without
my mother pointing out errors in
my ways and pushing me toward
things I wouldn't have done on my
own.

I always feel better when my mom is around. I still like her to take me to my doctor appointments. I feel safe knowing she'll come in and talk to the doctor if they stop listening to what I'm saying or begin accusing me of things I've never done. She has spent hundreds of hours in hospitals with me, yet, she never complains and repeatedly tells me she'd do it all again in a heartbeat. That kind of love is hard to find and something I never want to take for granted.

I only pray I can be a fraction of the woman my mom is. I hope I show the same tender love and care for my children as she shows my brother and me. That I can be a faithful wife to my future husband and honor him as she honors my dad. I can't emphasize enough how fortunate I am to have the mother I do. I thank God daily for placing me in her womb and I pray that He will infuse her with extra strength as she continues to faithfully stand by my side.

Here are some poems I wrote for my mom to hopefully capture just a sliver of her being.

Mother

A mother's love
So sweet, it must be from above
A mother touch
So gentle, it means so much
A mother's devotion
No stronger emotion
A mother's sacrifice
No greater price
A mother's hands
So calloused, because she's taken a stand
A mother's voice
More than enough to suffice
A mother's knees
Worn from prayers, because she did not flee
Oh how can I thank my mother
For I can ask for no other
Words will never suffice
How can I even be precise
It would take many a year
To come even near

Thank you so much for being you
For being so true
For being here
Even when I wasn't near
For sticking close
When I needed it the most
For being kind
When I refused and was blind
I'll love you forever
I'll like for always
For ever and ever
MY mama you'll be!

The Mother

A baby lay in her crib fast asleep
The mother's tired, but happy eyes
gazed down on her little girl
She remembered the day her
precious child had been born
Though the process was painful,
the pain disappeared
When she held the new life in her
arms
The mother covered the baby with
a soft pink blanket
And she whispered "I love you"

The toddler lay in her bed
Her covers all askew
The patient mother smiled down on
her young daughter
She remembered the day her little
girl said "ma ma"
And crystal tears entered her eyes
She fixed the covers that were
twisted around her daughter
And whispered, "I love you"

The five year old lay on the ground
The pretty mother shook her head
She remembered when her little
girl had decided to cut her baby
doll's hair
And then learned it would not grow
back
The mother gently picked up her
little girl and laid her in her bed
And she whispered, "I love you"

Eight years old and tuckered out,
the girl is fast asleep
The beautiful mother gazed down
upon her daughter's pretty face
An illusion of a smile appeared on
her face

As she remembered her daughter
learning to ride her bike
And the several times she had
bandaged up a scraped knee
She patiently picked up the
blankets that had been kicked onto
the ground
She covered her daughter once
again
And she whispered, "I love you"

The ten-year-old girl lay in her bed
The hot summer night had caused
her to kick off her sheets
The air was cooler now and the girl
was curled into a ball
The mother stood nearby
She smiled when she remembered
the joy that her child had
When she had gotten her ears
pierced by her dad
Then the mother covered her child
And she whispered, "I love you"

Thirteen now, the teenage girl lay
in bed
The blankets had been twisted
about due to the restlessness the
teen had experienced

Her mother stood in the room and
gazed upon her daughter
She smiled and thought *I have
begun a new adventure
The teenage years
They can be either years of joy and
learning or years of sadness and
separation*
Then the mother covered her
daughter with the warm blankets
And she whispered, "I love you"

At fourteen, the girl was still awake
Studying for school
The mother walked in the room
and said, "Now time for bed...
okay"
The daughter gave her a curt little
nod and said, "Soon mom I'm
almost done"
The mother sighed and left the
room for she was tired too
She lay in bed and she thought
about the past year
She smiled when she thought
about how beautiful and precious
her daughter was to her

She just wished her daughter
thought the same way about
herself
The smile disappeared as she
thought about how her daughter
had changed
The happy go lucky toddler had
been replaced by a mellow teen
She no longer covered her
daughter up
But she still loved her with all her
might
And so she whispered, "I love you"

Making it all better

The girl lay in bed thinking
She thought about the years
She thought about the
Struggles
Laughter
Fun
Sadness
Anger
And yet through all those years
one thing had stayed constant
Her mom's presence
Making it better

She remembered the times she
had scrapped her knees
And who would be there
But her mom
To comfort her as she cried
To kiss the cuts
To bandage them up
To make them better

She remembered the times when a
pet died
When the grief was so hard to bear
And then she realized she didn't
have to bear it
Cause her mom took her in her
arms
And held her as she cried
And made everything better

She remembered the times when
hunger was so strong
When she thought she was
starving
Yet who was there every day
making meals
Who was there to feed her when
she was hungry?
Her mom making it all better

At other times she was sick
So sick that she couldn't get out of
bed
Yet who stood by her bedside
Not concerned about her health but
about her daughter's
Bathing her head in cool cloths
Holding her hair as she puked
Giving her broth and water
Whispering words of comfort as
she cried
It was her mother
Making it all better
She remembered the times when
she was bored
When she wanted to find
something fun to do
When she couldn't do it because it
was too far away
And who would take her but her
mom
After the event she would say mom
did you have fun
Her mom would answer saying I
wasn't doing it for me I did it for
you
She was sacrificing her time to
Make it all better

At other times things were wrong
The girl didn't want to say what
She would sit in stony silence
Or cry silently to herself
Yet one person always noticed
And asked her what was wrong
She might say nothing
Yet the person would persist
Or just hold her
Or just comfort her
Who was it?
Her mom of course
Making it all better

At other times the girl struggled
With weight
Or with stomach pain
Or with other things
Yet her mother was there
Carting her to doctor's offices
Holding her tightly when things got
overwhelming
Telling her words of
encouragement to keep her going
Making sure she succeeded
It was her mom
Making it all better

The girl lay in bed and a tear slid
down her cheek
She realized she was loved so
much
Yet at times she took it for granted
At times she didn't recognize what
her mother did for her
At times she didn't acknowledge
everything her mom did
Yet she was honestly and truly so
grateful
She was so glad and so she got up
out of bed
Walked to her mom's bedside gave
her a light kiss on the cheek
Whispered I love you
And said thanks mom for
Making it all better.

Rishe

August 10, 2014

This essay is dedicated to Kevin Fox, my brother.

I rubbed the sleep from my eyes and sifted through my three-year-old brain, trying to figure out what I was supposed to remember about today. A light bulb went off in my head and I jumped out of bed, momentarily startled by the petite figure of my grandma entering my room.

"Is mommy okay?" I asked her concerned.

"Your mother is just fine and so is your new baby brother!" she replied, a smile dancing across her lips.

"When can I see them?" I demanded.

"Soon" she promised.

My little heart burst with excitement. I had a baby brother! The baby would be in *our* house and I'd get to take care of him, play with him, and life could only get better from here.

The day my little brother was born was one of the best days of my life. It was the day my best friend was born. I treated him as if he was my own child. If he cried, my heart would break because I hated to think of him being in pain. I became glued to my mother's side, helping her feed him, bathe him or change his diaper. He claimed a space in my heart the day he was born and he will always have a place there.

When we were little, he couldn't pronounce my name, so I became Rishe. I have no idea where he came up with that, but it's a title I bear with honor. He was my partner in crime and if he called me, I'd come. We fought off bears, robbers, and dragons together. We made castles, forts, and hide-a-ways. We crafted our own language and would communicate in it, much to the bewilderment of those surrounding us. We had a secret code of knocks. We wrestled, climbed trees, and rode bikes together. Sure we had disagreements, but our love was stronger than any fight, and we became inseparable.

I was also his official taste tester. When we were little, he wouldn't eat anything Rishe didn't eat. If I tried something and decided it didn't taste good then he wouldn't even bother sampling it. I grew up with several food allergies forcing me to avoid fruits, tomatoes, candy, cake, apples and several other things. When we went to parties, I'd always be the loner not eating cake or ice cream. However, when my best friend came along, I was no longer the only one not participating in the birthday dessert. Now, my partner in crime would sit right next to me eating pretzels or Pringles, instead of the ice cream and cake because he had deemed the dessert unacceptable since Rishe wasn't eating it.

Memories of our childhood are ones I'll forever cherish. From mud fights to seeing who could find the most snails to keep as pets, we were in constant competition with each other. However, if it we were in a competition against other kids in the neighborhood, we'd become the team to beat. We did everything together. Bath time got even better because now I had someone to play with in the tub and the water fights would commence. I no longer had to resort to using a doll for dress-up because now I had my own personal model. I also had more toys to play with because, let's be real here, any toys he got immediately became fair game for me to play with. Life definitely became better than I could've imagined when my little brother entered my world.

Yet, he too has been through a lot because of me. Remember all those doctor appointments I've had to go to over years? The doctor appointments that last twenty minutes, but you wait three hours for? Well, he came to each and every one of them until he was old enough to stay home alone. When I was hospitalized, he gave up his weekends to come visit me. By that point, he was a teenager, in high school, with plenty of other activities he could do on the weekends. Instead, he sacrificed all that to come to the hospital to hang out with me. He has never liked being in hospitals because he doesn't like to be around medical equipment or see people being treated. Yet, he put aside his fears to come be with me. His weekends were his favorite days of the week because he'd get to go to the skate park or hang out with friends, but he sacrificed all that to be there for me.

I remember one time when he was at the hospital with me they had to replace my IV. He left the room, but before he exited he looked sternly at the nurse and told her she couldn't hurt me and she'd better do a good job. He didn't let his fear stop him from protecting his sister.

Just as I have always guarded him, he also protects me. I've never felt fear when I have him standing by my side. Once, I used to be bigger and stronger, but now the roles have switched. He towers above me and when he wraps his strong arms around me, all feels right in the world. I know without a shadow of a doubt that he'd put himself in harm's way, in order to save me, just like I would do the same for him.

My biggest fear growing up was that he'd also suffer from my disease. I begged God to keep him safe. I actually think I prayed more that he wouldn't get the disease, than I prayed for my own healing. God graciously answered my prayer. Why did I pray that? Mainly for selfish reasons. I can't stand to see that kid in pain. I used to get mad at my parents for spanking him. Once, when he cursed, and my mom washed his mouth out with soap, I went and washed my own mouth out with soap because I didn't want him suffer alone. This is why I say my prayers were selfish when I prayed for his deliverance. They were selfish because I didn't want to watch him go through what I have endured. I can't imagine the pain he struggles with since he has had to watch me suffer.

Let's look at this from his viewpoint. His only sister, whom he has spent all of his life with, is falling apart in front of him. The doctors can't seem to fix her. She appears strained and distraught with life. When she feels really ill, she gets frustrated and angry with him. She looks sick and frail. Her eyes hold oceans of pain. She is his sister. The girl he first loved. The girl he never wants anyone to hurt. Yet, there is nothing he can do to alleviate the anguish she deals with on a daily basis.

Despite all this, he has never wavered in loving and supporting me. I have heard many stories of siblings who become detached from their sick sibling, but my brother has *never* done that. He continues to be there for me regardless of how sick I am. He continues to invite me to parties or events with his friends, not caring that I'll attract attention because of how I look or because I'm carrying an IV around with me. He has sacrificed work, school, and his time to be there for me.

When he came down to UF for my graduation we had a blast. It was the best weekend I had at UF. Right before he left I asked him if he was glad we got to go to some local hangouts so that the trip was still fun and not only a boring graduation ceremony. He replied by telling me he came down to Gainesville for the sole purpose to see me graduate. He wanted to see me accept the diploma I fought hard for. He was happy we got to "party," but even if we hadn't he would've been happy. He was there to support me during my graduation. The wisdom and significance of those words touched me deeper than he'll ever know.

During the summer of 2014 he worked at a camp a few hours from our home and I hardly saw him. One day he came home, surprising all of us. When he walked in that door, all felt right again in the world. Tears streamed down my face as I wrapped my arms around him and refused to let go. This is the impact this kid has had on my life and will continue to have. If he weren't here I'm unsure where I'd be in life, but I know I wouldn't be where I am right now. I have loved

him since the day he was born and
I won't stop loving him.

Poems I wrote for him.

My Baby

From the first day
That I could play
I wanted a friend
That could bend
Or set new trends
Not just one that was stuffed
Or that could be fluffed
And that's when you came
Forever claimed
As my lil bro

As soon as I was able
I held you like you were from a
fable
Vowing from then
To let no harm or bad men
Hurt you in any way
Because at that moment as you lay
You became my baby to stay

As you grew I always would hold
your stubby hand

Making sure if you fell I could help you withstand
The rough ground that could scrape you up
We always were so picturesque never to breakup
As we grew we fought
Growing slightly apart and distraught
But always I would fight for you
Because you were my baby
For any who dared to hurt you made me so angry

And now you may be taller
And a whole bunch stronger
But I'll never stop worrying
Or caring
Or being willing to die
So that you might still fly

Yet now I find that you are holding me
When I have no strength you listen to my silent plea
You embrace me so gently
As I once did to you so aptly
I'll never stop loving you
For you will always be my baby bro

And no one can ever change that
fo sho

Brother

Ever since your birth
From that day you entered this
earth
You have always been my little one
And made my life lots of fun

I've protected you like a treasured
star
Because in reality that's what you
are
And no matter if we are separated
by many a mile
My love for you will last a very long
while

For years I've yelled at anyone who
dared to hurt you
Because those who upset you, did
damage to me too
And still I have your back
A promise in which I won't slack

But now you have mine too

And the bond we share is felt by
few
Cause now I look to you for help
For you come running if I yelp

You are so much stronger and
bigger than me now
And when my friends see you, they
all say, "wow"
But you just use your strength to
protect me
To make me feel safe, you see

Now you treat me like a priceless
jewel
And hurt all, who to me, are cruel
I trust you with my very life
For I know you treat me, like you'll
treat your wife

When you are near I feel safe
I surely don't need my mace
For your strong arms defend me
And you never charge a fee

Thank you little one
For helping me out a ton
For being my protector
My little brother forevermore

A Second Family

May 8, 2014

I walked because I was told to. I sat because I was told to. I could only listen. I was a robot obeying the directions of those surrounding us. They were dressed in brightly colored orange and blue gowns. We wore black gowns as if we were headed to a funeral. In essence we were going to a funeral of sorts. For we were about to say goodbye to a significant chunk of our life. A solid four years. The only way I held it together was through complete denial. I went through the motions like a robot. I merely listened to what they told me to do and followed the person ahead of me. I shook on the inside. My soul felt lost. Graduation was an accomplishment. However, I wanted nothing to do with crossing that stage. I wasn't ready to say goodbye to the last four years of my life. More important, I wasn't ready to say goodbye to the people who had started out as friends, but were now family.

All week, I was a mix of raw emotions. The only emotion I understood was not wanting to graduate. I wanted nothing to do with graduation. A lot of people couldn't understand. They would say, "You've been through more than anyone else these last four years. You've fought harder for a degree and you've worked your butt off! Why are you upset?" They almost considered me ungrateful. I wanted to tell them they had no right to judge me. They couldn't possibly understand what went on inside me, if, even I, couldn't understand. I wanted to cherish my last week in Gainesville and I wanted to be with those who truly meant the most to me. At times, I felt like locking myself away in my studio apartment, but deep down I wanted to be with those I treasured. At times, my emotions overwhelmed me and I broke down in tears and completely fell apart. I was also determined not to waste the precious time I had left with those whom I only had superficial relationships.

Academically, my last week in Gainesville meant studying for the last finals I'd take as an undergraduate student at UF (University of Florida). Usually, I was annoyed and frustrated when I had several finals during finals week. This meant the semester would drag on longer. However, this year, I fully embraced it. First, studying for finals kept my mind occupied and off the pressing matter of my upcoming graduation doom. Second, finals meant there was still something preventing me from leaving UF. I seriously debated skipping my last final or leaving it blank so I could fail. Of course once I got to the exam, I couldn't bring myself to leave it blank, but I had definitely studied less than normal. During that week my brain operated on a different track than it normally did.

Socially, my week consisted of cherishing the college nightlife and there was not a night that week were I was let down. Those rumors you hear about the University of Florida being a good time may have some truth to them—just sayin'.

It was easy to manage my nightly adventures because I couldn't sleep that entire week. I had a few nights where I'd sleep three to four hours and then I'd be wide awake. Adrenaline, anticipation, dread, and an emotion I still can't name coursed through my veins, keeping me awake like caffeine never could. I'd lay in bed for hours thinking about my hazy future. Sadly, my health had utterly crushed my plans for immediate admission into PA (Physician Assistant) school.

When I wasn't thinking about my future I'd reminisce. Memories of the last four years would flood my brain. Memories—so priceless, precious, and powerful they'd leave me breathless. I recounted how many times God worked His perfect timing. How could I begin to tell Him how grateful I was for the people He brought into my life these past four years? During my time at UF, I met a lot of people and made many friends. However, most important, I made friends who became family.

During one of these last nights in Gainesville, I explained that concept to my parents. In high school I had friends who I called family, but those friends were different than the friends I called family here. In high school, I had my actual family (my mom, dad, and brother) only a phone call or ten- to fifteen-minute drive away. Here in Gainesville, my family was more like a twenty-five-hour drive away. Therefore, if I had an emergency I had to rely on a friend and that is how some of my friends became family. I knew, without a shadow of a doubt, if I picked up the phone and called any of them to ask for help, they'd be there in seconds to minutes. It didn't matter if they were studying for a major exam or if they had just pulled an all-nighter and needed sleep or if they didn't feel well. If they knew KFox, as I was known to some of them, or Kristen, as I was known to others, was in trouble, they'd be there.

You can't assign a numerical value to that type of friendship, for it's priceless. Most of these friends were associated with my UF club lacrosse team. I knew I could call anyone at Wheat house (the nickname given to the house they lived at), or any senior and they would be there for me. The other major group was my neighbors that I lived around my junior and senior years.

A distinguishing characteristic between my friends and my friends who became my family was the way they treated me. As my health declined and I became sicker, my body began to mirror my illness. My healthy and vibrant frame became thin and weak. While, my heart and spirit have stayed alive and full of light, this light couldn't mask how strange I appeared to many. Yet, my friends who became my family never hesitated in inviting me out to restaurants, bars or clubs with them. They never hesitated in including me in group photos or introducing me as their friend. Just because I didn't look good didn't mean they would disown me. They looked past the superficial and into my soul and that's what made them truly amazing. The fact that they stood up for me and accepted me, regardless of how my appearance changed, made a greater impact on me than they will ever know. It also gave me the drive and determination to continue my studies at UF, and hence, graduate with a degree in four years. Many told me it would be impossible for me to graduate in just four years, because of everything I was experiencing with my health, but I learned long ago nothing is impossible with God.

As my health declined, there were people who distanced themselves from me. While that was hard and disappointing to accept, I understood why. They did it to protect themselves. They protected themselves from the pain of losing me if something were to happen. They also protected themselves from the social awkwardness that sometimes occurs when you're around me. You see, people often stare at me when I have to carry my feeding tube around or they stare because of how I look. So, for those other friends, it was easier to withdraw from the relationship than invest in it. To those who have responded this way, I harbor no bitter feelings. I choose to forgive them, for I realize they did it to shield and protect themselves. When I see them, I still greet them with a smile. What good would it do to stay angry at them?

To conclude, I did walk across that stage. Although, I was dazed and my motions robotic, I successfully walked, without tripping, I may add. And, on May 3, 2014 I officially became a graduate of the University of Florida. I wouldn't have finished my degree if the friends I call family had not been there. Their support helped me emotionally, physical and psychologically to successfully complete my degree. Now don't get me wrong, I also had the support of my family. They were my number one cheerleaders, but they had to cheer from twenty-five hours away. I could call them crying, but I couldn't cry on their shoulder. I couldn't get a hug from them. I couldn't have a physical conversation with them or touch them. This is why my friends who became family played such an integral role in my success. They filled that role my family usually filled, but couldn't at the time. I hope these friends grasp the impact they've had on me. I couldn't have graduated without them. If they read this, they will hopefully gain a small sliver of understanding and they will realize how much they've meant and how they'll always have a special spot in my heart.

Acknowledgements

I'm writing these acknowledgments on November 27, 2014 or Thanksgiving 2014. It makes sense then that today I recognize and thank those who've helped me in my battle. The people who gave me hope to continue to fight. People congratulate me for continuing to fight for myself, but I shake my head and merely laugh when I hear this. You see, if I used myself as a motivation to keep fighting, I wouldn't fight anymore. I would be in Heaven, for there I would be living in a place with my Savior where I wouldn't experience any pain or sickness. I haven't fought for myself because I long to be in the presence of my Savior. No, I fight for those I love and who love me, those who don't give up on me, when I give up on myself. Those who've impacted my life in ways they'll never understand. You see, if I didn't have these people in my life, I wouldn't be alive, and so to them I owe a debt that can never be repaid.

First and foremost, I want to thank God for giving me the ability to write. I majored in Health Science and minored in Spanish. I am planning on going to Physician Assistant School. Hence, I haven't completed many writing or English courses, yet here I am publishing a book. This confirms the fact that God gave me the ability to pour my heart out on paper, so others may find hope through my suffering, thoughts and emotions. Also, I'm so thankful that Jesus has held me in His strong arms, for if He didn't hold me, I'm not quite sure I'd make it through each and every day.

Second, I want to thank my wonderful family. You'll never know how hard it is to watch a family member suffer from an illness until it happens to someone in your family. I selfishly thank God that I'm the one who suffers because I can't imagine how difficult it would be to watch one of them go through what I go through. I firmly believe that my family has experienced more than I have for they have watched me suffer. They've seen their child fall apart, writhe in pain and become incredibly sick. They have told me numerous times that, if they could, they'd take away my disease so I could be free. I can't imagine what they go through on a daily basis or the pain they've suffered on my behalf. However, I know that without their constant love and support, I would have given up long ago. I have NEVER spent a day alone in the hospital or ever gone to a doctor's appointment alone. My mom, Cynthia Fox, has spent hundreds of hours sitting in the hospital, with me, for appointments, tests and/or surgeries, and I never heard her complain. My father, Tim Fox, accompanied me when my mom wasn't available and has given me countless "scratch-backs" a.k.a.

back rubs, as I moaned in pain and agony. Thank you, Mom and Dad for all you've done and continue to do. Without you being there I know I wouldn't be here.

Last but not least, my brother, Kevin Fox, has been a trooper through all of this. I'm lucky to have him as a sibling. I've prayed more for his health than for my healing because I was afraid he would become sick like me. It terrified me because I didn't want to see him suffer. Yet, for most of his young life, he watched me suffer and has never let me suffer alone, even when it was hard and confusing for him. When we were children, he used to be my little shadow, following and imitating all I did. Now we're older and have our own lives, but he still makes sure I'm doing okay and checks to see if he needs to beat someone up for me. He is my best friend. I love you to the moon and back little one.

Not only have I been blessed with an amazing immediate family, but God has also blessed me with an incredible extended family. When I was in the hospital two years ago (2012), my relatives, in and around Colorado, came and visited me, offering a lot of support and encouragement. This shout-out goes out to you Aunt Kay, Uncle John, Mary, Sam, Jenny, Jessie, John, Annie, Tommy, and Granddad. Furthermore, I want to thank Aunt Kay for being my faithful pen pal these past three years.

I want to thank the Snow Mountain gang, who has faithfully supported and prayed for me through the years. The Wells family (Becky, Kaitlyn, Kyle, Amanda, and Michael), the Sheffler family (Theresa, Henry, Margo, Madaline, and Matthew), the Lucas family (Mary, Sam, John, Jenny, and Jessie), Annie Gisphert, and Aunt Kay and Uncle John Gispert. Even though I may only be there for a twenty-four-hour stint, I never fail to feel the love and I continue to feel the love through the texts, letters, and gifts you still send my way. Thank you.

I am indebted to my cousin, Zack Fox, who lived with my family for a couple months. He absolutely hates anything medically related. Nevertheless, he didn't let that fear stop him from loving me, and on a few occasions he spent the night at the hospital with me. That takes incredible guts and I'll never forget him doing that for me.

Thanks to another cousin, Joseph Fox, I will forever live on in video game world. He is a wiz with computers and is currently designing his own video game. I'm one of the characters in the game (who wears an orange and blue hat—Go Gators!). He created this character to heal others because he knows my passion is to help anything or anyone that is suffering. That meant so much to me!

A shout-out to my dad's brothers, their wives and children, who regularly pray for, support, and love me in their own special way.

This shout-out goes to my mom's brothers, sisters, their children and my grandma. Thank you for the love and support you send my way. Your cards, care packages, and phone calls have helped me keep my head up.

To my surrogate grandparents, thank you for adopting me as your own grandchild. Gramma and Grampa Huffman thank you for constantly sending me cards and care packages, which have brightened my darkest days. These gave me energy and hope to continue on. Grandma and Grandpa Kenaston thank you for the cards and care packages you've also sent. They were rays of sunshine that broke through my clouds of depression and sadness.

I want to especially recognize my Grandma Kenaston (Mel Kenaston) who faithfully printed out my essays, edited them and mailed them back to me. Additionally, she and Grandpa Kenaston (Casey Kenaston) have helped support my publishing venture. Without their support, this book would not be possible.

To Dr. Rogers. He is the one doctor who hasn't given up on me. He hasn't labeled me with an eating disorder, like most other doctors. He has faithfully stayed in contact, no matter where I've lived in the country. Many people dream of having a doctor who is compassionate, caring, and considerate. However, with Dr. Rogers I didn't have to dream for he's really like that. He epitomized the concept of good bedside manner. Even when I moved from Virginia, where I originally met him, he'd still call and check on me. I am only saddened by the fact that I can't have him as my primary doctor for the rest of my life. I also want to give a shout-out to his nurse, Luz Nazareno for coordinating appointments and quickly responding to any emails I sent her.

A big thank you to Amy Cordova, who is my nurse case manager, here in Colorado. Whenever I have an issue with medication refills, referrals, finding providers, etc., Amy has solved the problem with lightening speed. She has gone above and beyond in all she has done for me. Many nurses would benefit from her example.

To my friends in Virginia: I know I left you in 2010, but many of you have stayed in touch and continue to nurture our friendship. To Mama Gross, Lauren Boenau, Jenn Hogan, Cassie Smith, Lauren Brindley, Taylor Crosson, Dawn Xiang and Carly Salas thank you

243

for the letters and care packages.
To Sofia Herrera and Alice Yu,
thank you for not only sending me
letters and gifts, but also visiting.
Your visit is one I will always
cherish and remember fondly.

To Meghan Neary, thank you for
taking time out each day to text
me. I enjoy our texting
conversation that began November
of 2012 and has continued until
this day. Thank you also for the
gifts you've sent me and for taking
time out of your busy schedule to
come visit me in Colorado, it
meant so much to me. Never
forget you are a member of our
family.

To my Companion Family: Dr.
(Mamma) Christopher, Dr.
Margolis, Dr. Ainspan, Connie,
Stephanie, Molly, Diane, Kathy,
Elizabeth, Michael, Mike, Bob,
Rashana, Ashley, Scott, and
Lindsay thank you for helping me
grow into the person I am today.
I'll never forget my first job and

the people who made it so wonderful. Last but not least, I want to give a special shout-out to Charlotte and Doug Bavely, who made me a member of their little family. They opened their home to me and included me in their little pack. They let their dogs, Hank, Tyson, Boop, and Dutch, love me to pieces. Furthermore they always made sure I was comfortable, happy, and provided for whenever I stayed at their home.

To my friends in Florida: Graduating from the University of Florida (UF) wouldn't have been possible without my Florida friends. I needed to know that if I had an emergency there were people I could call to come help me when I needed it. To the group of people I hung out with all four years of college, I will never forget our rush parties, party bus adventures or club escapades. Thank you for not only including me in your lives, but also letting me come stay in your homes during various breaks. This shout-out goes out to you Savannah, Morgan, Kara, Lindsey, Emily, Emmy, Ariana, Rachel, Lauren, Garrett and the others who were there for some part of those four years.

To my lacrosse team. I can't convey the appreciation I have for you. I have NEVER known a more amazing group of girls than you. From my freshman to my senior year the people on this team blessed me. My freshman year, I knew nothing about lacrosse, but I wanted to try out a new sport. I walked up to their information table where Katie Weisz encouraged me to come out and try. I did! Under the patient tutelage and support of Sarah Sarnoski, Lauren Lapp, Brittini Peck, Nicole Nadeau, Marissa Higgans, and Kate O'Linn I learned to play. Even though I was easily the most inexperienced freshman out there, they still included me in the Freshman Herd (shout-out to those who lasted until senior year

[McKinley, Nicole, Brooke, Katya and Christine]). The group was created by the one and only McKinley Carden (who later on, nicknamed my IV pump The Generator, to make it seem like it came from the world of superheroes versus a hospital). My sophomore year I wasn't even at school, but the team saved my jersey number, and sent love and support my way throughout the entire year. My junior and senior year I was on the team, but was too sick to play. This didn't matter to these girls, they allowed me to travel to games, stand on the sidelines and be included in team activities. I can assure you that my life wouldn't be the same if I hadn't joined this team.

I want to give a special thanks to Jenna Hildabrand, Katie Weisz and Sarah Sarnoski for taking time out to teach me about lacrosse plus love and support me. These girls continue to text to make sure I'm okay and send me love and encouragement when I'm down. I'm incredibly honored to have these three as close friends and love them to death.

Another incredibly special person, who was also part of the team, is Nicole White (Bebe). She started at UF the same year I did. Honestly, when I first met her I was deathly afraid of her, but I soon learned the heart she possesses is incredible. During our sophomore year, when the team took their trip to Santa Barbara, Bebe created a cardboard cutout of me and brought "me" on the trip. Throughout the week, she posted pictures on Facebook of "me" doing various activities with the team. What she didn't know was that I had been in the hospital for over a month and was at the end of my rope. However, this gave me the strength I needed to not give up. It was an act that seemed simple in her eyes, yet meant the world to me. Furthermore, as the years passed she continued to stick by my side, supporting and loving me in many different ways. I'm honored to call her a friend and I'm not quite sure what I would do if she weren't in my life. I will cherish her forever and always.

This shout-out goes to the Alinas. These girls, who were also on the lacrosse team, included me not only in their lax lives, but also their normal lives. I will never forget the times I've flailed with these girls. From Grog's mucky muck to New Orleans's Bourbon Street, I've shared countless adventures with them and cherished every minute. Thank you, Jackie (Jack) Schaefer, Stephanie (Steph) Peck, Katie (Kat) Sonier, Dani Kleinberg, Sally Sue (Kelly) Nicholson, Kim Mockel, Nicole (Bebe) White, Brianna (Bri) Blum, Abigail (Abby) Sarnoski, Alina (Lini) Ayoub, and Kristen (Carnz) Carney. Even in Colorado I'm connected to them because we are in one big group text together—a group text that keeps me from being lonely, sad or depressed.

My next shout-out goes to my roomies. I lived in a studio apartment my junior and senior year; however this didn't prevent me from having roomies (people living around me). So this is to you Mike Spegele (aka big brother), Robert Montgomery, Chris Hogan, Travis Weber, Jenna Demczak, Spencer Polling, Sam Beatty, Sarah Sada, Lissette Portocarrero, and Ashley Hunt.

To two guys who are like brothers to me, this shout-out is for you. Michael Star, thank you for the prayers, the love you send to me, and your numerous gifts. I'm so glad I met you at the end of my freshman year. You have blessed me in so many ways. I can never repay you. Billy Vann, thank you, for making sure I didn't have to bike to the store when I didn't have a car down at school. For driving to Orlando to pick me up so

I didn't have to pay extra money to fly into Gainesville. For letting me do laundry at your house so I could save my quarters. I love you so much! Thank you for being you and being not only my friend, but also my brother.

To Derek Hunt, thank you for being my own personal paramedic and helping me with anything life, health- or school-related. Not only did you drive me around to different places or change out my feeding tubes, you also encouraged me and found ways to make me smile when smiling was the last thing I wanted to do. You were first my teacher, but then became a friend and now you are a big brother, holding a special place in my heart forevermore.

Thank you to the countless professors and advisors who supported and encouraged me throughout my years at UF. Dr. Young, Dr. Julian, Dr. Shectchman and Mrs. Burns you four went above and beyond for me so many times and I cannot thank you enough for that.

Last but not least, to the people in my home state of Colorado, this shout-out goes to you. In 2010, I came to Colorado with my family and then left for college a week after we arrived. Therefore, I didn't know anyone in Colorado when I returned from school after my freshman year.

The very first friend I made out in Colorado was Erica Emanuelson. I met her before I became sick, yet even after I became sick she didn't leave my side. She always knows what to say to make me smile or laugh.

I want to extend my deepest gratitude to Adam and Kellyn Rolfe, who've opened up their home to me and let me use it as a refuge, escape or a place to relax and chill. The depth of their love and support are immeasurable.

Adam hates hospitals, yet he still came, with Kellyn, to visit me and that spoke volumes. Kellyn supports and encourages me in ways only she can. She is someone I have deep discussions with about life and someone whose opinion I trust and rely on. I'm thankful God brought this amazing couple into my life.

Another person, in Colorado, who has made an incredible impact on my life, is Jared Sylvester. The care, love, and concern, he extends to me, cannot be measured. When I was in the hospital, he drove up most nights (a 120-mile round trip) and brought movies with him so we could watch them together. Let me remind you, I was in the hospital for more than a month! Furthermore, he continues to love and support me. I am forever indebted to him.

I want to thank two girls I met when I worked at Target, who have both impacted my life. Jourdan Squires is always on the lookout for fun things to brighten my day or add a little spice to my life. Furthermore, while I was in the hospital, during 2012, she had orange bracelets with blue lettering made that said" We Love Kristen Fox, Just Stay Positive". She proceeded to pass these bracelets out to countless people, giving me hope as she dispersed them. I'll always remember our shared bowl of mac n' cheese. The love and care she has shown me and continues to show me has touched me deeply!

I have never met someone quite like Lydia Armstrong and there is no one who could ever take her space in my heart. We may not talk for months at a time, but every time we do we solve half of the world's problems, so I'd say we're pretty efficient. She has always said, that to her I'm just Kristen. I'm not Kristen who is sick or Kristen with health problems. To her, I'm Kristen, the person she loves and cares about, and who means the world to me.

I want to thank Megan Andersen, the girl I work with, for covering work shifts for me when I've had doctor appointments or other conflicts. She is not only a co-worker, but also a friend and I'm blessed to have her in my life.

To two people who recently became friends, Abigail (Abi) Spears and Michelle Mendelsohn. Thank you for your friendship, support and love I've felt in just the short time we've known each other. Abi you're my tea soul mate and I'm excited to share this love with you. Michelle, from pumpkin patches to other random adventures, I'm glad you're in my life to bring smiles and remind me that when life gets tough, you have to get tougher.

To the staff at Focus on the Family, thank you for your encouragement, love, and support, even when I'm not volunteering. I can't adequately express my gratitude for Ketty Kerns who has let me become her shadow when I'm at Focus. She has and continues to help me with this publishing process. She also assists me in my Spanish learning and faithfully prays for me. Bruce Peppin and Marianne Hering have both sacrificed their time to help me with this publishing process and I'm indebted to both of them.

To Brianna Peppin, who also has health struggles similar to mine, may God continue to give you strength and victory in your own journey; never give up!

I met Ashley Franken because God brought us together. He knew we were meant to be soul mates and I needed someone to teach me about marketing. I want to thank her for the impact she has already made on my life and the impact I know she will continue to make.

Molly Greenwald is the incredible artist who designed the cover of this book. Thank you so much, girl! Your talent takes my breath away.

I want to extend my deepest gratitude to Mrs. Gosnell, who volunteered to read over each of my essays and edit them for me. Thank you for sacrificing your time to contribute to my success.

Last, but not least, I want to thank my editor, Krishana Kraft, who carefully edited my work and helped me publish the book you have in front of you. Without her help, I would not be as well off.